Green Mountain Club

Snowshoeing in Vermont

A Guide to the Best Winter Hikes

First Edition

The Green Mountain Club
Waterbury Center, Vermont 05677

The Green Mountain Club, Inc.
4711 Waterbury-Stowe Road
Waterbury Center VT 05677
802-244-7037
www.greenmountainclub.org

Book design by Sylvie Vidrine

Edited by Mary Lou Recor and Chris Hanna

Maps compiled by William Toussaint and Daniel Currier

Front cover photo: Mount Mansfield looking toward Smugglers' Notch.
Photo by Alden Pellett.

Back cover photo: A well packed trail heading up Wantastiquet Mountain.
Photo by Jeff Nugent.

First Edition
2005
ISBN 1-888021-15-2

Contributors

This guide would not have been possible without the contributions of the following volunteers and GMC staff members: Rolf Anderson, Richard Andrews, Katie Antos-Ketcham, Pete Antos-Ketcham, David Blumenthal, Michael Chernick, Scott Christiansen, William Clark, Patricia Collier, Kate Darajky, Larry Dean, Marcia Dunning, Renee Durham, Llyn Ellison, Marge Fish, Keri Foster, Jonathan Frishtick, Julia Grand-Doucet, Steve Grant, Carol Gregory, Dave Hardy, Ruth Hare, Phil Hazen, Paul Houchens, Jenn Karson, Anneliese Koenig, Steve Larose, Matt Larson, Brynne Lazarus, Paul Moffat, Matt Moore, Dorothy Myer, Jeff Nugent, Andrew Nuquist, Reidun Nuquist, Luke O'Brien, Herb Ogden, Tia Patterson, Alden Pellet, Sylvia Plumb, Peter Saile, Wendy Savoie, Susan Shea, Lexi Shear, Mary Spayne, Val Stori, Jonathan Szalewicz, Sylvie Vidrine, Greg Western, and Kevin Williamson.

CENTRAL VERMONT
CAMEL'S HUMP

OTHER REGIONS

SOUTHERN VERMONT

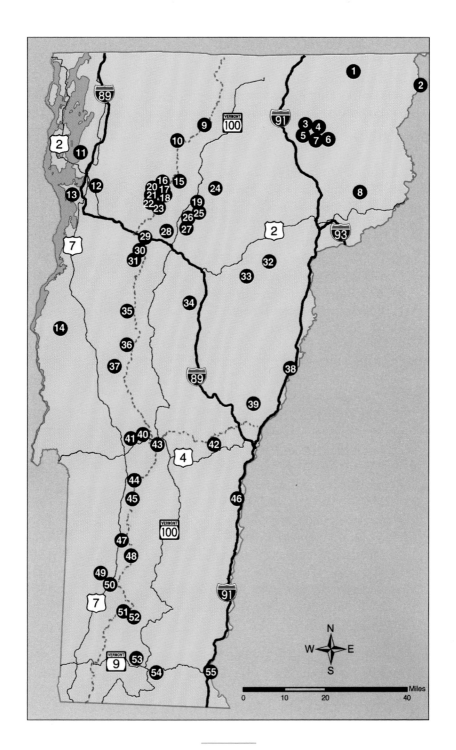

Introduction

Hiking in the Vermont winter can be pure joy. The trails are uncrowded. The lack of leaves on the trees makes distant views possible. Black flies and mosquitoes are a faded summer memory. And the bonds that form between hiking companions can turn into life-long friendships. Still, winter offers more than its share of challenges. The trails can be icy or invisible under a cover of deep snow. Trail markers can be obscured by wind-blown snow or completely buried. Driving to trailheads on slippery roads can be hair-raising. Summer parking areas may be unplowed and additional hiking miles required just to reach the beginning of the trail. Cold temperatures make regulating body heat especially difficult. Despite these challenges, or perhaps because of them, snowshoeing treks can be among your most enjoyable. The maps and detailed descriptions in this guide will take you to the best winter trails in Vermont. The rest is up to you.

Notes on using this guide

The hikes in this guide are organized by regions of the state, then north to south within each region. Some are near cities and towns, others are in the heart of the mountains. They are all day hikes.

The mileages are one-way unless otherwise noted. We have not included difficulty ratings or estimated hiking times because, in winter, both depend on trail conditions and snow depth, which varies considerably from December to March and between northern and southern Vermont. Relatively easy hikes can be challenging after a heavy snowfall and difficult hikes can seem easy if the trail is well-packed by other snowshoers.

Before heading out on any of the outings, it is important to consider elevation gain, distance and probable trail conditions. How much snow has fallen recently? Has there been a thaw and then a freeze, possibly creating an icy trail? What is the forecast for your planned hiking area? Are trail conditions in the mountains likely the same as those in the valleys? April is still winter above 3000 ft.

Each hike description is accompanied by directions to the winter trailhead and a map of the trail and surrounding area. There are exceptions, such as Mt. Mansfield or Camel's Hump, where we have combined several hikes on one map. We recommend purchasing a Vermont road atlas for assistance in finding trailheads.

We selected the hikes with lightweight aluminum snowshoes with attached crampons in mind. However, wooden snowshoes or snowshoes without crampons are appropriate for many of them. A very few hikes may require the use of full or instep crampons. This is included in the description.

We have noted where the winter trailhead parking area differs from the summer lot due to snowplowing, or lack thereof. This information is the best available at the time of publication and may vary from year to year.

While most of the trails are paint-blazed, blazing does not guarantee an obvious route to follow. Wind-blown snow plastered against a tree trunk can hide even the most well meaning blaze. Blazes that appear at eye level in the other three seasons can be at knee level or completely buried. Remember, if you lose the trail or are unsure which way to go, turning back and retracing your steps is always the right decision.

Be Safe

- Prepare before you go. Practice putting on and adjusting your snowshoes at home where it's warm so you won't spend time figuring out the bindings in the cold. Pack the night before and double check that you have all you will need.
- Tell a reliable person where you are going, when you are due to return and whom to call if you do not return on time.
- Travel with experienced hikers, especially when you are new to winter hiking. You will benefit from their knowledge and there is safety in numbers.
- Hike the trail in summer so you know the route before you hike it in winter.
- Set a turnaround time and stick with it.
- Carry enough gear to stay warm and dry if you are out longer than expected, especially in cases of injury or other emergency. Consider carrying a sleeping bag and bivy sack
- Take a wilderness first aid course and know what to do in an emergency.
- Carry two flashlights or headlamps. Keep the batteries warm or they won't work in cold temperatures.
- Be aware of spruce traps at higher elevations. When heavy snow falls, air pockets form under evergreen branches. When you step on what looks like solid snow, you can sink up to your waist or neck.
- Bring more food than you think you will need.
- Allow enough time for your planned hike, keeping in mind that there are fewer daylight hours in winter.

Be Considerate

- Take up as little parking space at trailheads as possible. Snow pack often limits parking space. Avoid parking on curves (where another car can slide into yours) or blocking driveways, plowed roads or gates.
- Walk to one side of cross-country ski tracks.
- Avoid post-holing by wearing your snowshoes.
- Pick up and carry out trash.
- Limit your use of toilet paper.
- Use privies whenever possible or cover human and dog waste with snow at least 200 ft. from the trail and water sources.
- Keep your dog under control. Be aware of ice buildup on paws.
- Avoid walking on alpine plants.

Before you go

This guide is not a course in snowshoeing techniques, winter safety, first aid or proper dress. The best way to learn safe outdoor winter travel is to take a workshop or connect with experienced hikers or groups. The Green Mountain Club offers workshops at their headquarters in Waterbury Center. The club's individual sections schedule winter outings led by experienced hikers throughout the state. GMC outings are a great way to learn about snowshoeing and meet people with similar interests. The following recommendations are based on years of winter hiking experience in various climate conditions. What you decide to wear or carry will depend on your own experience and comfort.

FABRICS – Even on the coldest winter day, you will sweat. Cotton clothing that feels cool against your skin in summer will feel clammy in winter. Once it gets wet, it stays wet and it will suck the warmth from your body, increasing the risk of hypothermia. Synthetics such as polypropylene are less absorbent, dry more quickly and will keep you warmer. While wool is better than cotton, it doesn't work as well as the synthetics. Even your Skivvies should be synthetic.

DRESS IN LAYERS – Regulating heat and moisture is the number one safety concern for winter hiking. The best way to control moisture, heat and body comfort is to dress in layers. Start with polypropylene underwear next to your skin, then add a body-fitting polypropylene shirt and pants (long underwear). Next don a synthetic fleece jacket and add a windproof

When Traveling in a Group

- Wait for all members before leaving the trailhead.
- Keep the person behind you in sight.
- Stop at trail junctions and stream crossings to wait for those behind you.
- Take your turn at breaking trail.
- Be willing to help other members to the best of your ability.
- Be sure everyone is back at the trailhead before leaving.
- Be sure all vehicles start before leaving the parking area.

hooded jacket and pants (preferably waterproof and breathable). Other essential clothing is a hat or balaclava, a scarf or neck gator, gloves or mittens and socks, all in either polypropylene or wool, and a pair of windproof shell mittens. Wearing layers will allow you to take off and put on clothing as needed. It is common to stop two or three times during the first hour of a hike to remove layers. We recommend you carry an extra set of dry clothing (shirt and pants) and dry mittens or gloves to change into, especially if you sweat heavily. On especially cold days or days when you expect to be out all day, we recommend carrying a fiberfill or down jacket.

BOOTS – In general, there are two options for winter hiking: rigid plastic boots with an insulated liner or pack boots with a waterproof rubber bottom, leather upper and wool felt liner. Plastic boots give more foot and ankle support and are water resistant. Pack boots allow for easier walking on hard surfaces, but are more difficult to fit with crampons. There are other winter boots on the market, including insulated overboots that can be worn over summer hiking boots. What you buy depends on what is comfortable and what will keep your feet warm.

PACK – Your pack should be large enough to carry the extra gear required in winter and have outside straps for lashing snowshoes, crampons and poles. You may want to tuck a small insulating foam pad into your pack for sitting on when you take a break.

WATER – It is important to replace body fluid lost through sweating, breathing and urinating. We recommend at least two quarts of water for a day hike. Hydration systems using a tube that runs from the water source to your mouth are susceptible to water freezing in the tube and blocking your supply. We recommend wide-mouth Lexan plastic bottles that can hold boiling water without deforming.

FOOD – Snowshoeing burns more calories than sitting in the recliner fingering the remote control, so it's important to eat high calorie foods throughout the day both to keep warm and to keep moving. The key to "feeding the inner fire" is to eat every time you stop, whether to drink, adjust layers or chat. Common winter hiking foods include chocolate, nuts, cheese, peanut butter, dried fruit, cookies and energy bars. This is not the time to diet.

POLES – Hiking poles provide stability and grip while hiking up and down steep slopes and through deep snow. They also work well for knocking snow from overhanging tree branches. The best and most expensive are collapsible so they can be stowed in your pack when you don't need them. On the other hand, discarded ski poles from the transfer station work as well.

ICE AXE – An ice axe may be necessary on Mt. Mansfield, Camel's Hump, Mt. Abraham and wherever the terrain is steep and icy. Before you carry an ice axe, learn how to use it.

SNOWSHOES – Although there are many brands of mountaineering snowshoes, they all serve the same two purposes: flotation and grip. They must keep you from sinking too deeply into the snow and they must give you enough grip to climb. Most have one cleat on the bottom under the ball of your foot; some have a second one under the heel. They have a

How to Keep your Water from Freezing

- Fill the bottle 3/4 full with room temperature water, then fill the last 1/4 with boiling water.
- Keep the bottle in an insulated bottle carrier.
- Place the bottle upside down in your pack. This will keep the cover from freezing on the bottle.
- In your pack, surround the bottle with extra clothing or keep it in a wool sock.
- Carry a small thermos of hot liquid (hot chocolate, tea, jello, etc.)
- Place the water bottle inside your fleece or shell jacket next to your body. Your body heat will keep it from freezing.

binding that attaches the snowshoe to your boot. It is important that this binding hold the snowshoe firmly in place. A poor quality or improperly adjusted binding will slip off your boot and you will lose your snowshoe. Inspect your snowshoes for wear and tear before you go out. The size of the snowshoe will depend on your weight; the heavier you are, the larger the shoe. We recommend trying several pairs before buying either by renting them or attending the Green Mountain Club's annual Snowshoe Festival where you can try several national brands for a nominal fee.

REPAIR KIT – Common repairs are broken bindings, poles or pack straps. We suggest carrying flexible wire, duct tape that sticks in the cold, thin nylon cord and even a spare binding (the neoprene equivalent of the traditional A binding fits most snowshoes). As with any breakdown in a remote area, sometimes you have to be creative.

FIRST AID – To your summer kit add sunscreen, extra batteries, a metal cup, a lighter, a small stove (for melting snow), chemical hand warmers, a flashlight or small headlamp, and an extra snack bar.

MAP AND COMPASS – Because winter trails are often harder to find and follow than summer trails, it is important to carry a good map, preferably waterproof, and a compass and know how to use them.

Emergencies
If you have access to a telephone, in emergencies, call 911 and the dispatcher will contact the appropriate rescue personnel. Keep in mind that cellular telephone reception is spotty in the mountains and cold weather reduces the performance of telephone batteries. You may also have to sit hours in the cold waiting for rescue. Your best equipment in an emergency is to prepare by taking a course in wilderness first aid or winter mountaineering.

Resources
Green Mountain Club
4711 Waterbury-Stowe Road, Waterbury Center, VT 05677
802-244-7037 • gmc@greenmountainclub.org

Adirondack Mountain Club Winter Mountaineering School
814 Goggins Road, Lake George, NY 12845-4117
518-668-4447 • winterschool.org

Northern Vermont

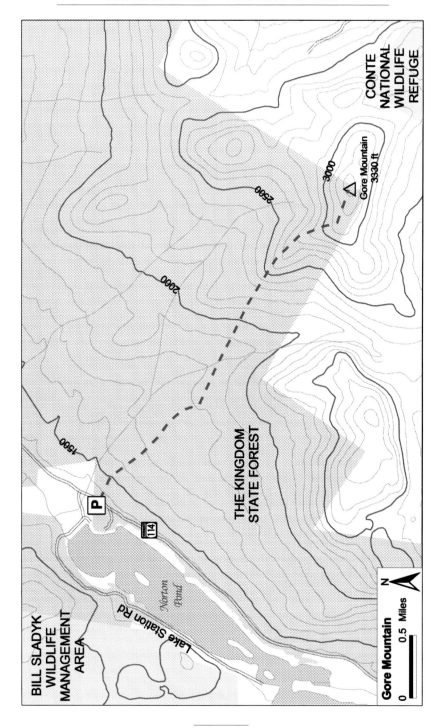

BILL SLADYK
WILDLIFE
MANAGEMENT
AREA

Lake Station Rd

Norton Pond

THE KINGDOM
STATE FOREST

CONTE
NATIONAL
WILDLIFE
REFUGE

Gore Mountain
3330 ft

3000

2500

2000

1500

P

114

N

Gore Mountain

0   0.5 Miles

① Gore Mountain

Location: Norton
Distance: 3.8 mi.
Elevation Gain: 1,972 ft.

Located about 6 mi. from the Canadian border in Norton, Gore Mtn. forms the northern boundary of the Nulhegan River Basin. It is a broad mountain with varying habitats: beaver meadow, young forest, thickets, mature forest and spruce-fir forest. This variety makes it a likely place to see moose, deer or snowshoe hare or at least plenty of animal sign. The snow is often deep and lasts into spring. The climb is gradual for the first 2.4 mi., but approximately 1000 ft. of elevation is gained in the last 1.4 mi., making this an ambitious snowshoe hike. The summit is wooded with limited views, but offers an excellent remote backcountry experience.

GETTING THERE: The trailhead is on Vt. 114 between Island Pond and Norton, 8.5 miles from the junction of Vt. 14 and Vt. 111. Although there is no maintained parking lot in winter, there is room to pull off on the west side of Vt. 114 between Lake Station Road and DeVost Road, across from the trailhead.

DESCRIPTION: From the trailhead (0.0 mi.), the white-blazed trail, built and maintained by the Northeast Kingdom Conservation Service Corps, enters the woods through a small opening directly opposite the pull-off. It follows an unnamed brook for a short way, then climbs gradually for the first mile away from Norton Pond along an old woods road, originally used to access the fire tower and cabin on the summit. The trail then levels, passing through a series of abandoned beaver meadows. The wooded summit of Gore can be seen in the eastern distance. Continuing eastward, the trail crosses two small brooks and skirts the northern edge of a beaver meadow. At the end of the thicket, the trail passes an old, rusted car on the right, then bears left at a signed junction (1.2 mi.) and crests a short knoll before dropping down to parallel a tributary of Station Brook (1.5 mi.). Crossing the brook, the trail emerges on the edge of an expansive logged area (1.6 mi.), meanders through young forest, turns northeastward and climbs to the top of a second knoll. At 2.0 mi., the trail turns right on a wide timber company road for 200 ft. before finding a white blaze on the opposite (left) side. It ascends more steeply to a junction with the Lookout Trail (2.1 mi.). From the junction, the trail turns left to a second timber road (2.4mi.), which is occasionally used by snowmobilers. Crossing the road, the trail climbs more steeply through open hardwoods along the northwest ridge with occasional views of Brousseau and Round Mountains to the north, Coaticook and the Eastern Townships of Quebec to the northwest, the Bill Sladyk (Hurricane) Wildlife Management Area lands in Norton and Holland to the west. Old skid roads in this area make it easy to lose the trail. At 3.0 mi., after passing an old skid road, the trail turns left and begins a more persistent climb to the spruce-fir forest of the summit, then turns eastward, finally emerging at the edge of the summit clearing (3.8 mi.). Here, the abandoned fire warden's cabin still stands, although most likely buried in snow, with the only access through the open porch windows. There are limited views of the Nulhegan River Basin to the south.

A wintery blanket of snow covers the trees and rocks.

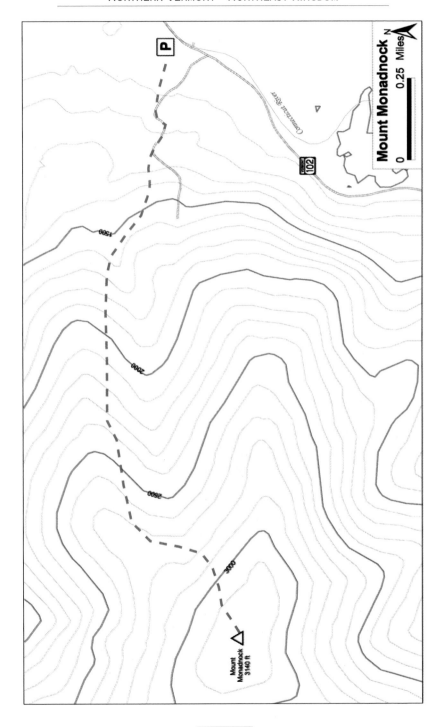

② Mount Monadnock

Location: Lemington
Distance: 2.4 mi.
Elevation Gain: 2,108 ft.

This remote summit with a newly renovated fire tower and the remains of the warden's cabin is seldom climbed in winter. The steps and platform for the tower were replaced by volunteers from the GMC's Northeast Kingdom Section in 2005, making it possible to once again enjoy panoramic views from the summit. This is an excellent destination for anyone seeking deep virgin snow, solitude and several hours of trail breaking. Although the trail is on private property, it is open to the public through the courtesy of the owner. Please respect this generosity by staying on the trail and keeping dogs leashed.

GETTING THERE: The trailhead is about 100 yds. north of the junction of Vt. 102 and Bridge Road (Lemington Colebrook Bridge) in Lemington. The trail leaves from a large sandpit on the west side of the road. The summer parking area is not maintained in winter, but there is room for about five cars in a pull-out 100 yards north of the sandpit on the east side of the road.

DESCRIPTION: The trail, marked with small signs, crosses the south side of the sandpit to a signpost, then turns left to cross an unmarked open field to a snowmobile corridor, which it crosses before entering the woods to the right of a wire fence. Following yellow parallelogram-shaped markers, it climbs a short distance through young forest with views east toward Dixville Notch, New Hampshire, then re-enters the woods and passes near and under several large rock outcroppings. The trail makes a sharp left, then climbs steeply just to the right of a brook. An old roadway leading straight ahead makes this turn easy to miss. The trail next turns right on a large abandoned roadway and climbs steadily along a brook on the right. From here to the summit, there are few trail markers. The trail/roadway reaches an open area with a small sign indicating a footbridge across the brook (1.8 mi.). As the trail enters denser woods, it becomes easier to follow as it begins a sustained climb to more open forest and the summit fire tower. The remains of the warden's cabin are 100 ft. beyond.

③ Westmore Town Forest

Location: Westmore
Distance: 1.25 mi. loop
Elevation Gain: Negligible

The Westmore Town Forest, which was a gift from the Lester Bill family, encompasses two beaver complexes, one abandoned and one active, a cedar spruce swamp and a bog. Volunteers from the Westmore Association laid out and maintain the trails; the Northwoods Stewardship Center NEK service crews built the bridges and the Vermont Youth Conservation Corps built the boardwalk. While the terrain is appropriate for beginners, the trails are not blazed for winter use and may be difficult to follow. Trail maps of the area, including Willoughby State Forest, are available free at the Westmore Town Clerk's Office Monday through Thursday.

GETTING THERE: From the north end of Lake Willoughby in Westmore, turn west on Peene Hill Road (Town Road #4) from Vt. 16 and follow it 1.0 mi. to a Nature Conservancy sign for the Town Forest. Park on the same side of the road as the sign. The trailhead is 40 ft. south of the sign.

DESCRIPTION: From the parking area (0.0 mi.), the blue-blazed trail leads southeast to follow the shore of the first, and larger, beaver pond. It turns east, passing south of two beaver dams, and reaches a junction with the Back Loop Trail (0.25 mi.). Bearing right, the trail skirts the second, and smaller, beaver pond, passing the dam on the left. It turns north-northwest toward the bog natural area. At 0.8 mile, the trail turns sharply left at a junction with the Back Loop Trail and comes to the bog boardwalk, which, in summer, allows a closer view of the variety of bog plants, including the rare pitcher plant. Returning from the boardwalk, the trail turns right at the Back Loop junction, passes along the east side of the bog (on the right) and returns to the junction with the route in (1.0 mi.). It then turns right to return to the parking area (1.25 mi.).

The Back Loop Trail skirts another old beaver pond and follows more hilly terrain across three bridges before returning to the west junction with the Bog Trail.

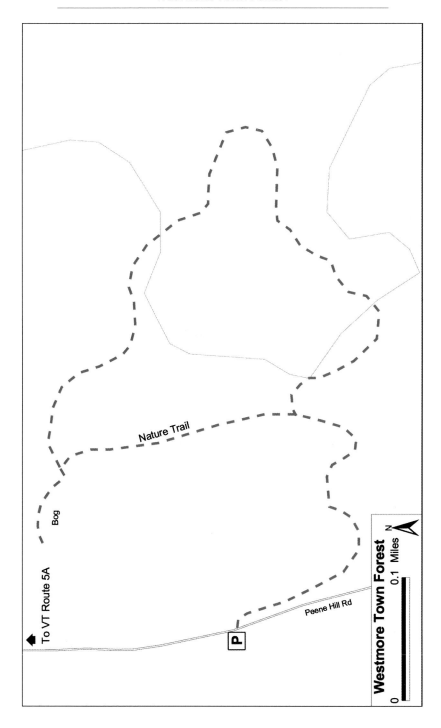

Westmore Town Forest

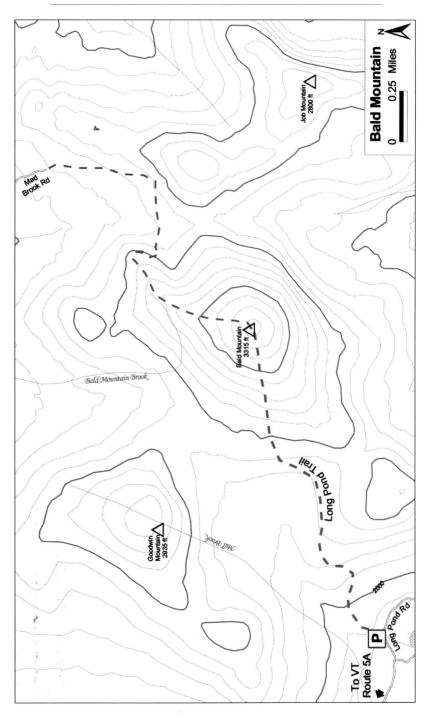

④ Bald Mountain

Location: Westmore
Distance: 2.1 mi.
Elevation Gain: 1,250 ft.

Bald Mountain (3,315 ft.) is the third highest peak in the Northeast Kingdom and provides one of the best views in the region from its recently restored fire tower. The two most heavily used trails to the summit, the Mad Brook (north) and Long Pond (south) Trails are maintained by the Westmore Association, the Northeast Kingdom Conservation Service Corps and volunteers from the Green Mountain Club. The recent acquisition of the summit property by the State of Vermont and its subsequent inclusion in the Willoughby State Forest has led to significant trail restoration as well as the complete renovation of the historic fire tower.

GETTING THERE: From Vt. 5A in Westmore, at the shore of Lake Willoughby, turn north on Long Pond Road following it for 2.0 mi. The trailhead is approximately 350 ft. on the left past the Long Pond fishing access.

DESCRIPTION: The blue-blazed trail leaves the parking area (0.0 mi.) and follows a gated logging road for 0.7 mi., bearing right at a junction and climbing moderately to an open log landing. It then leaves the far right corner of the landing and turns left into the woods where there is a sign for the Bald Mountain Long Pond Trail on a tree. The trail follows an old woods road before narrowing eastward into a well-worn (when not snow covered) path. The trail continues for some time through open hardwoods, then climbs more steadily into the subalpine spruce-fir forest. After climbing several steep pitches and passing a number of rock outcroppings, the trail emerges on the summit.

⑤ Wheeler Mountain

Location: Sutton
Distance: 1.3 mi.
Elevation Gain: 500 ft.

Although a relatively easy climb with little elevation gain, Wheeler Mtn. offers sweeping views of both Vermont's Green Mountains and New Hampshire's White Mountains. The view of Mt. Pisgah and Lake Willoughby is unsurpassed. Snowshoes with crampons are recommended due to the open rocky sections.

GETTING THERE: Five mi. south of the junction of Vt. 16 and U.S. 5 in Barton, turn left (north) onto Wheeler Mtn. Road. This one-lane, gravel road climbs steeply past Wheeler Pond (1.0 mi.) on the right and ends at the Wheeler Mtn. trailhead (2.0 mi.). The road is not plowed beyond the trailhead and limited parking is on the left, directly opposite the last house. It is recommended to ask permission of the homeowner before parking. The trail is not marked at the trailhead and, although it is on private property, it is open to the public. Please stay on the trail and keep dogs leashed. The trail is sparsely blazed and extra time may be needed for route finding.

DESCRIPTION: The trail begins to the left of two large maple trees in the parking area and passes to the right of a clearing through abandoned apple trees. It emerges in a second field and keeps to the right, entering the woods on the far end. (A red-dot blazed trail enters the middle of the field on the right, but is a more difficult route to the summit.) The trail, now marked with white dots, passes through an open hardwood forest and begins a gradual climb after crossing a small drainage. It skirts to the left of visible ledges, then makes a sharp right turn before beginning a steep climb. After another sharp right, the trail levels out before passing a series of open ledges and vistas to the southeast, including Wheeler Pond. From here, it enters the woods, crosses an area of open rock, then re-enters the woods on the eastern edge. The trail is now marked with white and red blazes. It emerges on top of the eastern cliffs with clear views to the east of Mt. Pisgah, Mt. Hor, Burke Mtn. and New Hampshire's Franconia Ridge. To the west, the Green Mountains loom in the distance from the Lincoln Skyline to Jay Peak. Beyond this lookout, the trail climbs gradually, entering the woods near the summit, then emerging at Eagle Cliff.

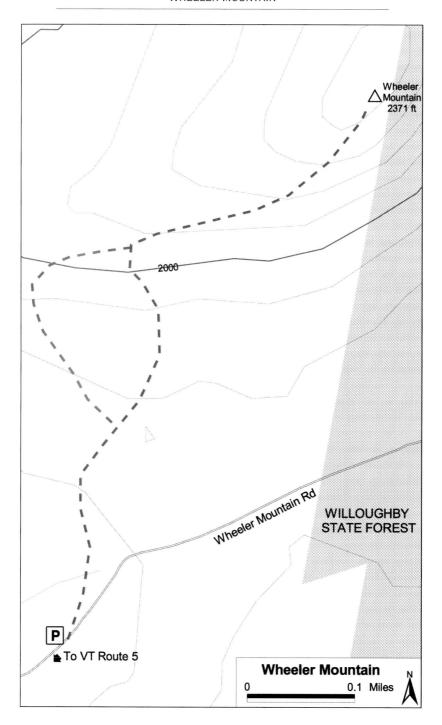

Wheeler
△ Mountain
2371 ft

2000

Wheeler Mountain Rd

WILLOUGHBY
STATE FOREST

P
To VT Route 5

Wheeler Mountain

0   0.1 Miles   N

A view of Mount Pisgah from Wheeler Mountain.

⑥ Mount Pisgah

Location: Westmore
Distance: 1.7 mi.
Elevation Gain: 1,450 ft.

The south trail to the summit of Mt. Pisgah is a popular snowshoe hike, therefore it is usually well-packed, requiring less effort than unbroken trail. In addition to views of Mt. Hor and Lake Willoughby from an open area near the summit, this route also offers several impressive viewpoints along the edge of the cliffs. Mt. Pisgah is located in the Willoughby State Forest, established in 1928.

GETTING THERE: From the south, the trailhead, located in Westmore, is on Vt. 5A, 5.6 miles from the junction of U.S. 5 and Vt. 5A in West Burke. From the north, it is 5.8 miles south on Vt. 5A from its junction with Vt. 16. Parking is available in a large pullout on the northeast side of Vt. 5A, marked Willoughby State Forest Trailhead, or at a state parking area at the head of a CCC road on the southwest side of Vt. 5A.

DESCRIPTION: The trail begins on the north side of Vt. 5A, at the south end of the large pullout and is marked with a sign reading: Mt. Pisgah, South Trail. It is well-marked with blue blazes the entire way. From the road, the trail descends an embankment and crosses a beaver pond on a boardwalk bridge. After following a small hogback ridge, it turns right to start uphill. Steeply climbing several switchbacks, it levels off to closely follow the cliff face. Several short spurs lead to dramatic overlooks with precipitous drops. These spots can be icy and should be approached with caution, especially when hiking with dogs and small children. The trail bears right and begins a steady climb to an open area near the summit where there are views south to New Hampshire's White Mountains, Victory Basin, Newark Pond and Burke Mtn. The trail leads a short distance further to the unmarked wooded summit. The North Trail continues north from the summit, eventually ending at the trailhead on Vt. 5A, 3.0 mi. north of the South Trail parking lot.

PLEASE REFER TO THE MAP ON PAGE 17

⑦ Mount Hor Overlook

Location: Westmore
Distance: 1.9 mi.
Elevation Gain: 200 ft.

The cliffs on Mt. Hor drop directly into Lake Willoughby, which at over 300 ft. deep is one of the deepest lakes in New England. It lies in a granite trough gouged out by glaciers more than 13,000 years ago. The Willoughby Cliffs are well known as one of the top ice climbing destinations in North America and ice climbers may also be seen negotiating the icefalls on Mt. Pisgah.

GETTING THERE: The parking area is located on Vt. 5A at the southern end of Lake Willoughby in Westmore. This parking area is not plowed in winter, however there is a pull-off large enough for several cars about 100 ft. from the trailhead across from an RV campground. This pull-off is shared by hikers, snowmobilers and people who are ice fishing. If this area is full, the Mt. Pisgah South Trail parking area is about a quarter mile south on the opposite side of Vt. 5A, although it is not always plowed.

DESCRIPTION: The blue-blazed trail leaves from the northern end of the parking area at a large kiosk (0.0 mi.). As there are several unofficial trails at this end of the lake, pay particular attention to the blazes. The trail turns left (west) before reaching the water, descends an embankment, then begins to climb the western side of Mt. Hor. At a signed junction (0.3 mi.), it turns left, climbs to an overlook and begins to traverse the side hill. The trail enters an open grove of mature hardwoods, mostly beech, maple and hemlock, where there are views of the Pisgah cliffs and Lake Willoughby through the trees. The footing here can be precarious due to the narrow sidehill path. The trail crosses a log bridge and continues at a gentle grade to the overlook at the base of the Mt. Hor Cliffs (1.9 mi.). The overlook sits 600 ft. above the lake and offers exceptional views of both Lake Willoughby and Mt. Pisgah.

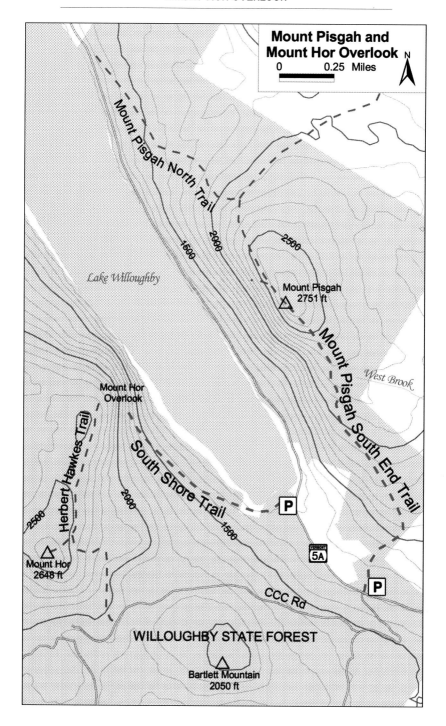

Mount Pisgah and Mount Hor Overlook

0   0.25 Miles

N

Mount Pisgah North Trail

2500

2000

1500

Lake Willoughby

Mount Pisgah
2751 ft

Mount Pisgah South End Trail

West Brook

Mount Hor
Overlook

Herbert Hawkes Trail

South Shore Trail

2500

2000

1500

Mount Hor
2648 ft

P

5A

P

CCC Rd

WILLOUGHBY STATE FOREST

Bartlett Mountain
2050 ft

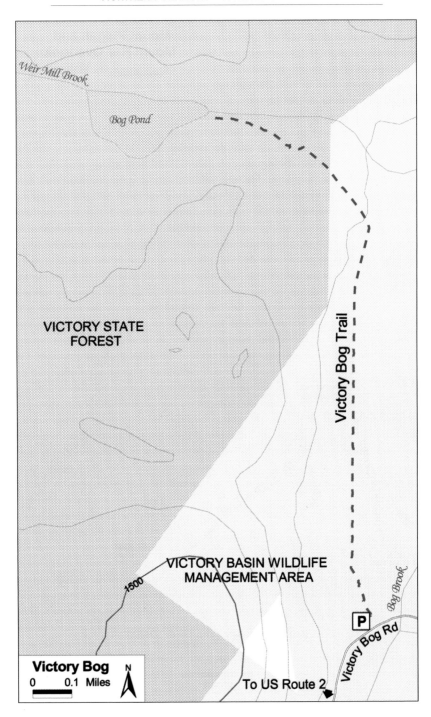

Weir Mill Brook

Bog Pond

VICTORY STATE
FOREST

Victory Bog Trail

Bog Brook

VICTORY BASIN WILDLIFE
MANAGEMENT AREA

1500

P

Bog Brook

Victory Bog Rd

Victory Bog

0   0.1   Miles

N

To US Route 2

⑧ Victory Bog

Location: Victory
Distance: 2.5 mi.
Elevation Gain: None

This moderate, quiet and beautiful snowshoe hike in the 4,000-acre Victory Bog Wildlife Management Area lies within the 16,000-acre Victory State Forest, which is open to various recreational uses. Evidence of moose, deer, coyote, fox and weasels is likely. There is no elevation gain as the trail wanders alongside the bog and through forests of cedar, spruce and fir. Because the trail is wet, it is best to hike it when there is adequate snowpack, keeping to the designated trail to avoid harming the sensitive bog vegetation.

GETTING THERE: From St. Johnsbury, take U.S. 2 east to North Concord, turn left onto Victory Road and follow it 6.0 mi. to the large parking area for the Victory Bog Wildlife Management Area on the left.

DESCRIPTION: The trail departs from the kiosk in the parking area (0.0 mi.). Although it passes in and out of woods, the first 1.5 mi. of the trail is mostly open, following beaver ponds on the left and the bog on the right. At the first junction (1.5 mi.), the trail bears left and enters the woods, heading toward Bog Pond. It then turns right onto a logging road and bears left at the first intersection, where the remains of an old foundation are on the left. Shortly thereafter, the trail passes the remnants of a stone dam. Bog Pond drains through this breached dam.

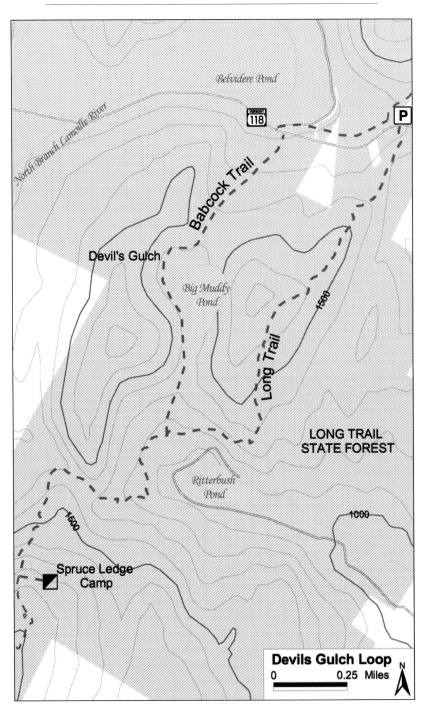

Belvidere Pond

North Branch Lamoille River

VERMONT 118

P

Babcock Trail

Devil's Gulch

Big Muddy Pond

Long Trail

1500

LONG TRAIL STATE FOREST

Ritterbush Pond

1000

1500

Spruce Ledge Camp

Devils Gulch Loop

0   0.25 Miles

N

⑨ Devil's Gulch Loop

Location: Eden
Distance: 5.0 mi.
Elevation Gain: 180 ft.

This loop hike includes a trip through Devil's Gulch where spectacular ice cascades form on the rock walls. Spruce Ledge Camp, at the most distant point on the circuit, is a fully enclosed shelter offering a nice lunch stop with a clear view of Belvidere Mtn. The last leg of the hike climbs through a small gap and follows the shoreline of Big Muddy Pond.

GETTING THERE: The trailhead is located at the Long Trail parking area on the north side of Vt. 118 in the town of Eden, 4.8 miles west of Vt. 100 and 6.1 mi. east of Belvidere Center. There is plenty of parking for the small number of winter trail users and the lot is plowed regularly.

DESCRIPTION: From the signpost and hiker registration box (0.0 mi.), the route heads south on the white-blazed Long Trail, crossing Vt.118 and entering an open hardwood forest, where it climbs steadily for 0.8 mi. In winter, there are views to the north of Belvidere Mtn. not visible in summer. The trail levels to a nice view over Ritterbush Pond (1.0 mi.), then drops steeply 500 ft. over the next 0.5 mi. This can be treacherous if icy, though in fresh snow it is a joyous downhill romp. The trail then parallels the shore of the pond, albeit at some distance, until reaching the junction with the Babcock Trail (1.7 mi.). Passing the junction, the Long Trail climbs gradually for 0.3 mi. where it enters Devil's Gulch, an awe-inspiring jumble of rocks and frozen water with one small stream crossing (2.0 mi.). Hidden holes covered by snow can make this section treacherous and hiking poles may be useful to probe before stepping. On the left, a frozen waterfall cascades 30 ft. from the rocks above, shimmering a blue color on sun-filled days. Although the Gulch is only 0.2 mi. long, it is worth pausing to enjoy the sights. Leaving the Gulch, the Long Trail climbs to a ridge and crosses a stream before reaching a sign for Spruce Ledge Camp (2.6 mi.). A blue-blazed spur trail leads 800 ft. to the top of the ridge and the shelter. A short distance from the shelter, Devil's Perch Lookout offers inspiring views of Ritterbush Pond and Belvidere Mtn., as well as the tailings from an old asbestos mine on the south slope of the mountain. From the junction with the shelter spur trail, this route backtracks through Devil's Gulch to the junction with the Babcock Trail (3.5 mi.), which it follows back to Vt. 118. The blue-blazed Babcock Trail ascends moderately along a stream to a height of land and Big Muddy Pond. It traverses the hill side, following the shoreline. There are signs of beaver activity at the northern end of the pond. Leaving the pond, the trail makes a long, gradual ascent to Vt. 118 (4.6 mi.), crosses the road and reaches the Babcock Extension Trail, also blue-blazed, which avoids the 0.4 mi. road walk. The extension briefly follows Edsel Rich Road, then, re-entering the woods, makes a brief, moderate ascent back to the parking area (5.0 mi.).

A restful spot for snowshoers on the trail to the top of Spruce Mountain.

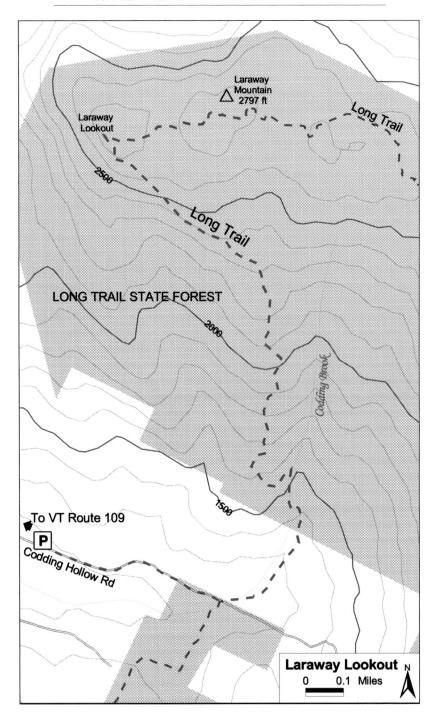

Laraway
Mountain
2797 ft

Laraway
Lookout

Long Trail

Long Trail

2500

LONG TRAIL STATE FOREST

2000

Codding Brook

1500

To VT Route 109

P

Codding Hollow Rd

Laraway Lookout   N

0   0.1   Miles

⑩ Laraway Lookout

Location: Waterville
Distance: 1.8 mi.
Elevation Gain: 1,390 ft.

Laraway Mtn. is a moderately challenging snowshoe hike to a vista offering views of the Sterling Range and Mt. Mansfield. In addition, in winter, the trail passes rock faces where spectacular ice pillars form, caused by the continuous runoff of water from the top of the mountain. Except for a short road walk from the parking lot, the hike follows the Long Trail marked by white blazes. These blazes can be difficult to see in winter.

GETTING THERE: From the junction of Vt. 15 and Vt. 108 in Jeffersonville, proceed north on Vt. 108 for 0.6 mi. and turn right on Vt. 109. Continue for 4.6 mi. to the village of Waterville and an additional 0.9 mi. to the Codding Hollow Road on the right. Cross the covered bridge and continue to a road junction, then bear left. After another mile, the road narrows at a farmhouse. There is a plowed parking area 0.1 mi. past the farmhouse on the right.

DESCRIPTION: From the parking area (0.0 mi.), the route follows the road for a short distance to the summer parking lot, on the left. The white-blazed Long Trail leaves from the far end of the lot, climbing modestly on old woods roads before crossing a stream and turning right to begin a steeper climb. Still remaining mostly on logging roads, the trail winds through deciduous forest before leaving the roads for good and entering birch-dominated forest. It bears west and begins to traverse the side of the mountain. The ledges are soon visible on the uphill slopes and, at the height of winter, veils of ice cascade down their faces. The trail climbs to the base of the ledges, then continues straight ahead, leaving the ledges for a short distance before climbing to another overhang, which it parallels. It then bears left and climbs moderately to the lookout. From this open rock, there are good views of the valley below, as well as south to the Sterling Range and Mt. Mansfield. For a longer outing, the Long Trail continues north from the lookout another 0.4 mi. to the summit of Laraway Mtn., where there are limited views. This portion of the trail is usually less obvious due to deep snow and is, therefore, less frequently traveled. The Long Trail continues north past the summit.

⑪ Eagle Mountain

Location: Milton
Distance: 2-3 mi.
Elevation Gain: 560 ft.

Eagle Mtn. sits on the shore of Lake Champlain, overlooking the Champlain Islands. It is relatively unknown and offers a quick getaway in populous Chittenden County. The property was conserved by the Lake Champlain Land Trust in 1995 and is managed by the Milton Conservation Commission. Only pedestrian recreation is allowed. The trails are well-marked and obvious and the terrain is suitable for beginners and children, as well as dogs.

GETTING THERE: From the US 7 bridge over the Lamoille River at the Arrowhead Lake Dam in the village of Milton, proceed north approximately 0.6 mi. and turn left on Lake Road. Follow Lake Road for 2.9 mi. to a farm and a left turn onto Everest Road. Continue 0.5 mi. to a stop sign and turn right. After 1.4 mi. (there is a red barn on the left), turn right again onto Beebe Hill Road. In 0.6 mi., turn left onto Cold Spring Road. Continue a short distance until the road turns left where the Eagle Mtn. trailhead is marked by a white bulletin board. Parking is available for 2-3 cars. Please do not block this private road.

DESCRIPTION: The trails on the Eagle Mtn. property are marked by green diamonds, numbered to correspond to the trail map on the trailhead bulletin board. The network of trails forms several loops and the numbering can be confusing. There are two main trails, one leading to the summit and the other to a beautiful lookout over the lake. The side trails are short enough that the best option is to simply wander about. A thorough exploration of the area involves a walk of no more than 2 or 3 mi. From the bulletin board, the main access trail follows an obvious old road, climbing modestly to a signed junction. To the right, a spur leads several hundred yards to the "summit" of Eagle Mtn. where there are limited views to the west. Straight ahead from the junction, the Hoyt's Lookout Trail continues about the same distance to a rock outcrop with a wonderful view over Lake Champlain and the nearby islands to New York and the Adirondacks. There are several well-marked side trails south of the lookout that make good options for the return to the trailhead.

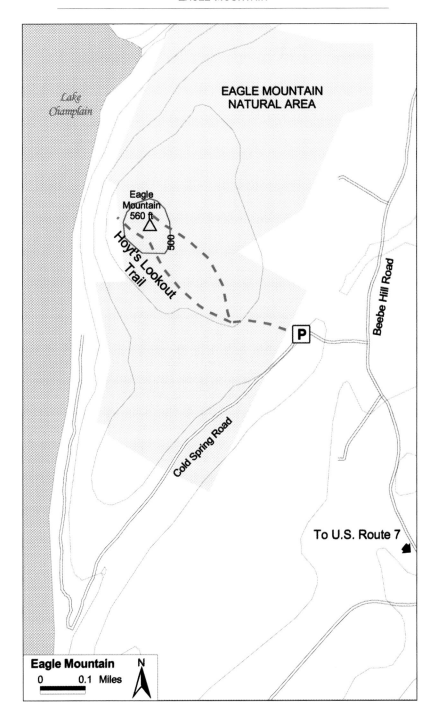

EAGLE MOUNTAIN
NATURAL AREA

Lake
Champlain

Eagle
Mountain
560 ft

Hoyt's Lookout
Trail

500

P

Beebe Hill Road

Cold Spring Road

To U.S. Route 7

Eagle Mountain   N
0   0.1 Miles

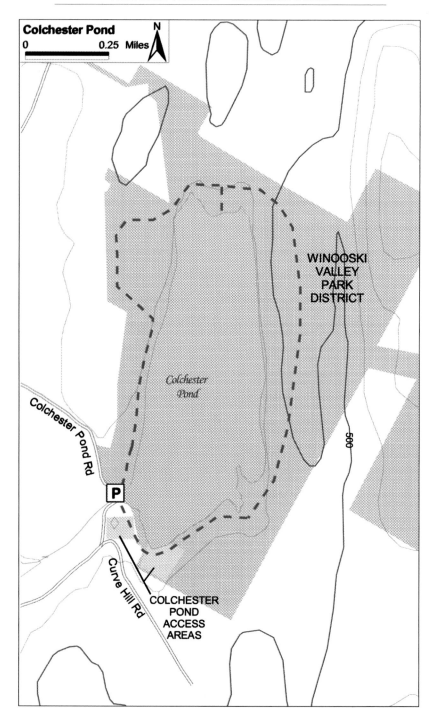

Colchester Pond

0 ——— 0.25 Miles

N

Colchester Pond Rd

P

Curve Hill Rd

Colchester
Pond

WINOOSKI
VALLEY
PARK
DISTRICT

500

COLCHESTER
POND
ACCESS
AREAS

⑫ Colchester Pond

Location: Colchester
Distance: 3 mi.
Elevation Gain: Mostly flat with some rolling hills

Colchester Pond is a peaceful wildlife preserve only minutes from Burlington. The Colchester Pond Trail circles the broad expanse of the pond, traveling through a nature preserve maintained by the Winooski Valley Park District. In some places, the trail provides expansive views of the pond and surrounding fields, with farm buildings and houses in the distance. In other places, it winds through intimate rocky ravines and thickly wooded peninsulas. It is easy to follow, since it mostly skirts the edge of the pond. In the woods, there are directional signs with arrows posted at potentially confusing spots. Occasionally, there are also diamond-shaped "WV" markers posted on trees. There are no restrooms or trash facilities and dogs must be leashed. For more information, call the Winooski Valley Park District at 802-863-5744 or visit wvpd.org.

GETTING THERE: From Vt. 2A in Colchester village, turn north at the traffic light on East Road, then right onto Depot Road in 0.2 mi. After crossing the railroad tracks, the road becomes gravel and its name changes to Colchester Pond Road. It crosses a one-lane bridge and the pond is on the right. The regularly plowed trailhead parking lot is straight ahead. The gate is open from dawn to dusk.

DESCRIPTION: From the trailhead (0.0 mi.), the trail leads straight toward the pond along a line of trees and shrubs near a meadow. At the shoreline, it turns north (left) in a clockwise direction. It then passes through a series of meadows separated by rows of trees and shrubs. Across the pond, there are dramatic views of rocky bluffs crowned by hemlocks and rising up from the ice of the pond's surface. Near the northern end of the pond, the trail enters a hardwood forest (0.5 mi.), moving away from the shoreline and climbing steeply for a short distance. It descends almost immediately through a stand of birches, rounds the northern end of the pond and touches the shoreline before climbing again. At a large white pine, a signed spur trail leads 0.1 mi. to the tip of a peninsula where there is a view south along the length of the pond. The trail descends to a bridged brook crossing, then begins a winding climb through rock outcroppings. It makes many sharp turns marked with signs and arrows and does not follow the shoreline. The trail flattens at a height of land on top of the bluffs that were visible from the first part of the trail (1.5 mi.). It continues on a straight, wide, easy-to-follow old woods road through dense hemlock groves. The trail descends to a meadow (2.3 mi.), crossing it to a visible break in the trees. It crosses a wide bridge with no handrails, crosses another meadow to a fence line, then follows the fence line west (right) around the south end of the pond. The trail hugs the pond here, almost like a tunnel through the snowy thicket of brushy plants and cattails. It then passes under the power line, coming out on Colchester Pond Road (3.0 mi.) and crossing the outlet for the pond on a single lane bridge. To the west of the road, a small water fall spills over the dam into a rocky, wooded gorge. The entrance to the parking area is immediately beyond this outlet (3.0 mi.).

A young snowshoer in Chittenden County.

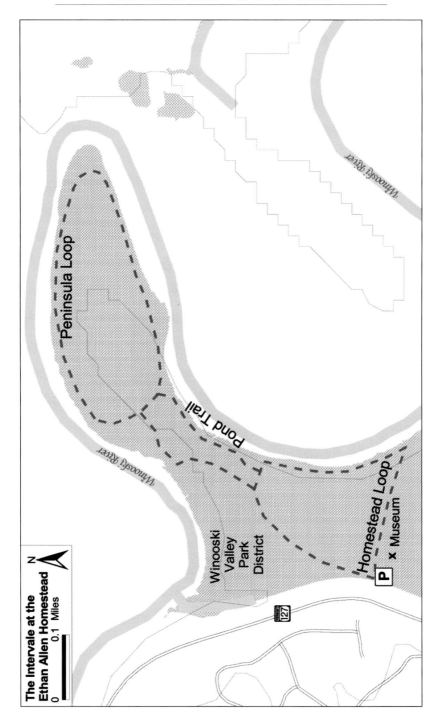

The Intervale at the
Ethan Allen Homestead

N

0   0.1 Miles

Peninsula Loop

Pond Trail

Homestead Loop

Winooski Valley
Park
District

x Museum

P

127

Winooski River

Winooski River

⓭ The Intervale

Location: Burlington
Distance: 2.5 mi.
Elevation Gain: None

Ethan Allen was the colorful and controversial leader of the fabled Green Mountain Boys who fought the British during the American Revolution to ensure Vermont's independence and future statehood. A museum and the restored 1787 Allen homestead contain a historical collection and interpretative exhibits of the time period. They are only open occasional weekends during the winter. For winter hours, call 802-865-4556 or check the website at ethanallenhomestead.org. The land surrounding the homestead is part of the Winooski Valley Park District, one of 17 natural areas with more than 12 mi. of shoreline along the Winooski and Browns Rivers, Lake Champlain and Colchester Pond. The park is open from dawn to dusk. Hot drinks are available if the museum is open. The trail is mostly unmarked, but open fields make route finding obvious.

GETTING THERE: From Vt. 127, also known as the Northern Connector or the Beltline, in Burlington, take the North Avenue/Beaches exit. Turn right immediately after the big curve (jug handle). Follow this road until the end, about 0.4 mi., at the Ethan Allen Museum parking lot. From Colchester, exit Vt. 127 at the North Avenue/Beaches exit. Turn left to pass over Vt. 127, then left again at the Ethan Allen Homestead sign.

DESCRIPTION: Facing the museum (0.0 mi.), the route begins on the left and soon passes the homestead, which sits on a bluff overlooking the Winooski River and Intervale. Two hundred yards beyond, the trail descends gradually toward the river. At the intersection at the bottom of the hill, it turns left to follow a row of trees planted to hold the soil along the banks of the wandering Winooski. At 0.9 mi., the Pond Trail leads 0.3 mi. to the back peninsula. It is often possible to see tracks of red fox, coyote, deer and fisher as well as the stripped bark and branches indicative of beaver activity in this area. At an open field, the beginning of the Peninsula Loop, the trail turns right to follow the river and circumnavigate the field. Near the end of the circuit, an opening in the treeline leads 0.3 mi. back to the outgoing trail and the return to the museum.

⑭ Snake Mountain

Location: Addison
Distance: 1.8 mi.
Elevation Gain: 900 ft.

Snake Mtn., conveniently located between Burlington and Middlebury, provides unobstructed views of the Champlain Valley with little effort. The mountain was named for its long, winding shape, rather than for any abundance of reptiles to be found there. In 1874, Jonas Smith built a hotel among the trees on top, away from the open ledges. There was also a 68-ft. observation tower that tourists could climb for ten cents. The mountain was renamed Grand View Mtn. for the hotel, but the hotel closed in 1925 and the name did not survive. The State of Vermont bought the summit in 1988 and most of the mountain is now part of the Snake Mtn. Wildlife Management Area. The trailhead, however, is on private property.

GETTING THERE: From the intersection of Vt. 22A and Vt. 17 in Addison, travel 2.7 mi. south on Vt. 22A to a left turn on Wilmarth Road. Follow this short road to its end at the junction with Mountain Road. The trailhead is straight ahead. There is a large parking area left (north) on Mountain Road about 500 ft. from the junction.

DESCRIPTION: The blue-blazed trail passes through a gate (0.0 mi.) onto an old road next to an abandoned red building. It is wide, relatively flat and often muddy in late fall, early spring or after a thaw. In 0.75 mi., the trail reaches a T-junction with an old carriage road and turns left, finally leaving the roadway at a Y-junction in 0.15 mi. The left fork of the Y ascends gently, then moderately on a sparsely orange-blazed trail, reaching the south shore of Red Rocks Pond at 1.5 mi. This tiny pond has no obvious inlet or outlet. The trail follows a ledge along the west shore of the pond, affording expansive views of the Champlain Valley and Adirondacks, then reenters the woods on the right at the north end of the pond. It climbs gently another 0.2 mi. to a junction with the dirt roadway. The trail now bears left (west) toward the lake and ends at a large concrete foundation (1.8 mi.) overlooking the valley. The true summit is in the woods to the northeast. To complete the loop, the return route backtracks east to the last junction, then leads straight ahead down the more traveled, but less scenic, dirt roadway back to the Y-junction.

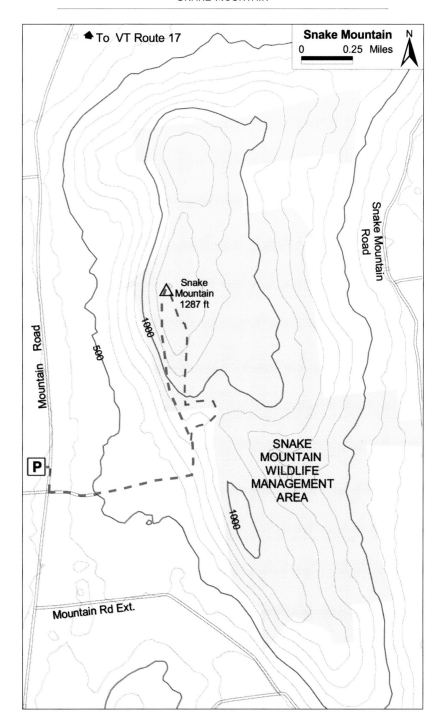

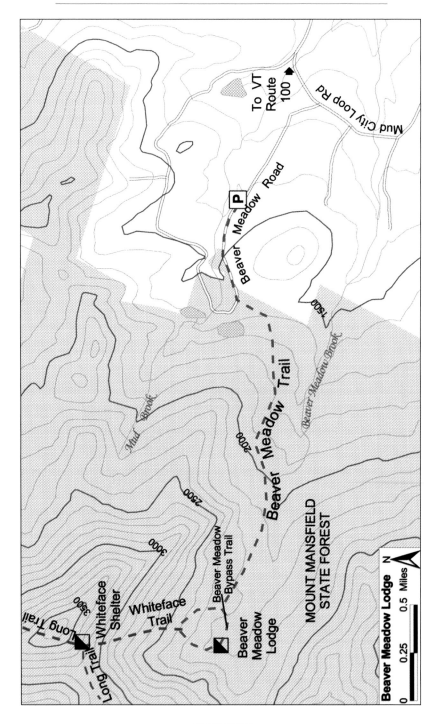

⓯ Beaver Meadow Lodge

Location: Morrisville
Distance: 2.3 mi.
Elevation Gain: 900 ft.

Beaver Meadow Lodge was built in 1947 by volunteers from the Sterling Section of the Green Mountain Club. The trail to it follows an old road-bed through mixed hardwoods and makes an excellent family snowshoe hike. On a clear day, it is possible to see Whiteface Mtn. to the north.

GETTING THERE: From Stowe village, follow Vt. 100 north to Old Stage-coach Road. Turn left and follow Old Stagecoach Road for 4.5 mi. to a stop sign at Morristown Corners. Turn left on Walton Road, passing Cote Hill Road on the right and Cole Hill Road on the left. At the next junction, turn left on Mud City Loop Road and follow it 1.8 mi. to a left turn on Rooney Road. At the next fork, turn right at the machinery shed on Beaver Meadow Road and follow it 0.7 mi. to the end where there is ample winter parking.

DESCRIPTION: The Beaver Meadow winter trail begins in the lower (southwest) corner of the parking lot and follows an old road approximately 0.5 mi. to a reddish gate on the left. Passing through the gate, the route continues on the roadbed up a moderate grade, crossing a VAST (Vermont Association of Snow Travelers) trail 0.3 mi. from the gate. It reaches the junction with the Whiteface and Beaver Meadow Loop Trails (2.0 mi.), which is well-marked by a sign. The Whiteface Trail continues straight ahead and the Beaver Meadow Loop and Chilcoot Trails, collectively known as the Beaver Meadow Loop Trails, bear left to Beaver Meadow Lodge. In front of the lodge, the trail narrows and becomes the Beaver Meadow Bypass Trail. The Bypass Trail loops around the meadow to re-join the Whiteface Trail. The Bypass/Whiteface Trail skirts the northern edge of the beaver meadow where the Whiteface Trail forks right. The Bypass continues left to climb a small hill above the meadow, then skirts the western edge before arriving at the lodge. To complete the loop, the trail continues southward in front of the cabin and across a drainage as it circumnavigates the meadow on its southern end, eventually crossing the meadow's outlet. It rejoins the Beaver Meadow Trail at the Whiteface/Beaver Meadow Loop junction.

⑯ Smugglers' Notch

Location: Stowe
Distance: 1.8 mi.
Elevation Gain: 560 ft.

The road through Smugglers' Notch is closed to car traffic in winter, which allows snowmobilers, skiers and boarders to use it as a connection to the parking areas and ski lifts at Stowe Mtn. and Smugglers' Notch Resorts. Ice climbers use it to access the icefalls at the top of the Notch. The road ascends gradually with views of the Mt. Mansfield ski area on the left and the Elephant's Head outcrop on the right. The caves in the Notch were allegedly used as a hiding place during the War of 1812.

GETTING THERE: From the intersection of Vt. 108 and Vt. 100 in Stowe village, follow Vt. 108 (the Mountain Road) west to the barricade just beyond the parking area for Stowe Mountain Resort, approximately 8.6 mi. from Vt. 100. There is ample parking.

DESCRIPTION: From the barricade at Barnes Camp (0.0 mi.), the un-plowed road climbs gently west past the trailhead for the Long Trail south on the left (0.7 mi.) and another trailhead and picnic area for the Long Trail north/Elephant's Head Trail on the right. After crossing a large culvert, it passes a small mound on the right, marking the drainage from the first slide on the Elephant's Head Trail above. At 1.3 mi., the Big Spring parking area and one-time site of a mountain hotel is on the right and the trailhead for the Hellbrook Trail on the left. The road narrows and steepens as it winds around large boulders that have fallen from both sides of the notch, including King Rock, a boulder that fell in 1910. It ascends through several hairpin turns and the horseshoe bend provides excellent views of the Elephant's Head cliffs and possible ice climbing activity. The hike ends at the Visitors' Center at the height of land in the notch (1.8 mi.). Although the center is closed in winter, it does provide a windbreak and resting spot.

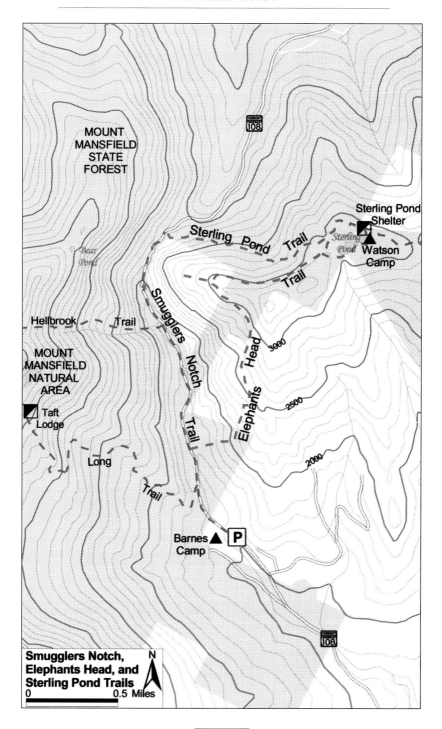

MOUNT
MANSFIELD
STATE
FOREST

108

*Bear
Pond*

Sterling Pond Trail

*Sterling
Pond*

Sterling Pond
Shelter

Watson
Camp

Hellbrook Trail

Trail

Smugglers Notch

Elephants Head

3000

2500

MOUNT
MANSFIELD
NATURAL
AREA

Taft
Lodge

Trail

2000

Long

Trail

Barnes
Camp

P

108

**Smugglers Notch,
Elephants Head, and
Sterling Pond Trails**

N

0   0.5 Miles

Snowshoeing up the Beaver Meadow Trail.

⑰ Sterling Pond

Location: Stowe
Distance: 3.3 mi.
Elevation Gain: 1,400 ft.

Although short in distance, this trail quickly gains considerable elevation and variable snow conditions can make the route icy and hazardous. Ski poles, crampons, full winter gear and steady nerves are often necessary. The trail is shared by backcountry skiers, snowboarders and hikers.

GETTING THERE: See driving directions for the Smugglers' Notch hike. This route may also be accessed from Jeffersonville. From Jeffersonville, follow Vt. 108 to the snow barricade past the Smugglers' Notch Ski Area, approximately 7.4 mi. from Jeffersonville, where there is ample parking. The top of the Notch is a 1.1 mi. hike up the closed road from the barricade.

DESCRIPTION: The trailhead for the Sterling Pond Trail (0.0 mi.) is located across from the stone Visitors' Center at the top of Smugglers' Notch (1.8 mi. from the barricade at Barnes Camp). Although there is a trailhead register, it is often buried in snow. From the register, the blue-blazed trail ascends a steep slope overlooking the notch, then continues north around a large rock outcropping, crossing a narrow gap above. Ice and wind-driven snow may make it necessary to select an alternate route around this outcropping. The trail then levels, crosses several drainages and continues almost in a straight line to Snuffy's Trail, a tractor road connecting the ski areas (2.9 mi.). From here, it is 0.4 mi. left to the outlet of Sterling Pond. The ski area usually grooms a trail across the pond, but care should be taken when crossing any body of water.

PLEASE REFER TO THE MAP ON PAGE 39

⑱ Elephant's Head Trail/Long Trail

Location: Stowe
Distance: 4 mi.
Elevation Gain: 1,780 ft.

In 2003, the Long Trail was routed off the road through Smugglers' Notch and onto the Elephant's Head Trail. Although the distance to Sterling Pond is not great, the trail is challenging as it traverses a side slope in places, crosses several slides, is often unbroken and can be difficult to follow due to the white blazes that blend with the winter landscape. From various points on the trail, there are clear views across the Notch to Mt. Mansfield and Taft Lodge.

GETTING THERE: See driving directions for Smugglers' Notch hike.

DESCRIPTION: From the barricade (0.0 mi.), follow Vt. 108 (closed) to the trailhead for the Elephant's Head Trail/Long Trail north (0.8 mi.) on the right. The trailhead is marked by a register, although it may be buried in snow. The white-blazed Long Trail crosses a small footbridge, turns left immediately before a closed log structure, then descends to a ford of the West Branch. This crossing can sometimes be difficult and snowshoers may want to seek out an alternative crossing down the stream bank, closer to the picnic area. After crossing a smaller stream, the trail bears right and ascends a long grade through beech and birch forest with intermixed fir trees and bushes, passing a beaver pond on the right. It climbs away from the stream via a series of sidehill switchbacks, requiring the kicking in of steps, then levels before reaching a series of rock ledges (1.5 mi.) with seasonal water flows crossing the path. Snow boarders and skiers use these drainages as off-trail descents from Spruce Peak. The trail continues uphill on moderate grades through a mixed forest of birch and maple to cross the lower portion of a 1985 slide, which reaches Vt. 108 only after an icy and precipitous descent (2.3 mi.). The trail climbs a sharp slope (snow usually covers the timber steps) to enter a boreal forest dominated by conifers (spruce, fir and pine) with snow-covered branches that often obscure the route. It crosses a second slide (2.5 mi.) with views across the notch to the ski slopes on Mt. Mansfield, the Adam's Apple and the Chin. The roof of Taft Lodge may also be visible. From this point, route finding may be difficult and require reliance on colored flagging tape left by trail adopters, branches clipped close to tree trunks, old blue blazes, brown paint covering the old blazes and, of course, the essential map and compass. The trail levels slightly (2.8 mi.), crosses a small stream and reaches a flat spot nearly above the second slide. The treadway narrows and reaches a spur trail at 3.3 mi. The 300-yd. spur trail ends abruptly at the cliffs above Smugglers' Notch and should be approached cautiously. Ice climbers on the cliff face below the overlook could be injured by loose snow or ice falling from above. The view includes a 1000-ft. drop into the notch, the sheer walls of the northern end of the Mt. Mansfield Ridge and the scar left by a 1983 landslide. At the spur junction, a marker indicates 0.7 mi. to the next trail junction. This distance is deceiving because increased snow depth and overhanging tree branches make route finding difficult. The trail crosses several boggy areas, ascends steeply to a saddle below Spruce Peak and reaches Snuffy's Trail (4.2 mi.), a lightly tracked road connecting the Spruce Peak Ski Area with Sterling Pond. Turning left, the Long Trail descends to a junction with the Sterling Pond Trail (4.5 mi.). From this point, descent is possible by returning via the Elephant's Head Trail or completing a loop via the Sterling Pond Trail to the top of Smuggler's Notch (see Sterling Pond Trail description), then Vt. 108 back to the parking area.

PLEASE REFER TO THE MAP ON PAGE 39

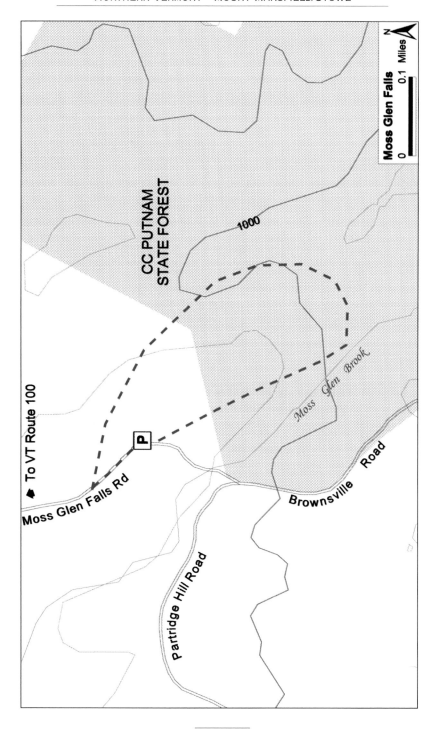

⑲ Moss Glen Falls

Location: Stowe
Distance: 0.4 mi., with other options
Elevation Gain: 150 ft.

The snowshoe to Moss Glen Falls offers winter hikers several options unknown in other seasons. Although just a few minutes by car from the center of Stowe, the trail presents opportunities for a loop hike through a spruce-fir forest with views of the nearby ski areas. The impressive falls showcasing the forces of water that have shaped this part of Vermont make this an excellent, quick getaway for a winter afternoon.

GETTING THERE: From Vt. 108 in the center of Stowe, follow Vt. 100 north three mi. to a "Y" intersection with Randolph Road. Bear right on Randolph Road to a right turn (0.4 mi.) at Moss Glen Road. Both cars and snowmobiles share this gravel road in winter. Turn left just before the bridge over Moss Glen Brook (0.9 mi.) into a parking area with a sign for GC Putnam State Forest, Burt Hollow Block, Moss Glen Natural Area.

DESCRIPTION: The route begins southeast from the parking area (0.0 mi.) in a large clearing marked by tall pine trees and cattails. It turns sharply right toward the banks of Moss Glen Brook and follows an unmarked trail through river birch and shrubs. Although winter conditions may make the trail difficult to find, it follows the streambed away from the road and parking area. It then curves away from the stream and climbs to a warning sign, where there are two options, either left to the cliff above the falls or right to stay at brook level.

Bearing left, south of the sign, the trail climbs steeply to the top of the cliff overlooking the ice-covered falls. It may be necessary to traverse the slope, making an "S" pattern, rather than climb straight up. Care should be used when approaching the edge of the cliff due to unstable ice and snow. Below the cliff, the brook runs through the ice, with stretches of open water sometimes visible. To the west are views of the ski trails on Mt. Mansfield and Spruce Peak, the Green Mountain Range to Madonna Mtn. and the ridgeline to the north. From the top of the cliff, the trail continues gradually upward to a grotto formed by hemlocks with only the muffled roar of the brook to break the silence. The views across the narrow gorge show uplifted, eroded granite carved over time by water from the brook. The trail levels at the top of the falls and ends at a junction with a snowmobile trail (0.4 mi.). It is possible to complete a loop back to the parking area by turning left on the snowmobile trail and left again on Moss Glen Road (1.0 mi.).

Bearing right, the path follows along the brook. Cantilevered rock walls extend along both sides of the brook, with a view to the trail on the cliff. Caution should be used as water sometimes undermines the trail. This short trail ends at the falls, where there are several downed trees and impressive views upward to the cliff face.

On the way to Moss Glen Falls, Stowe.

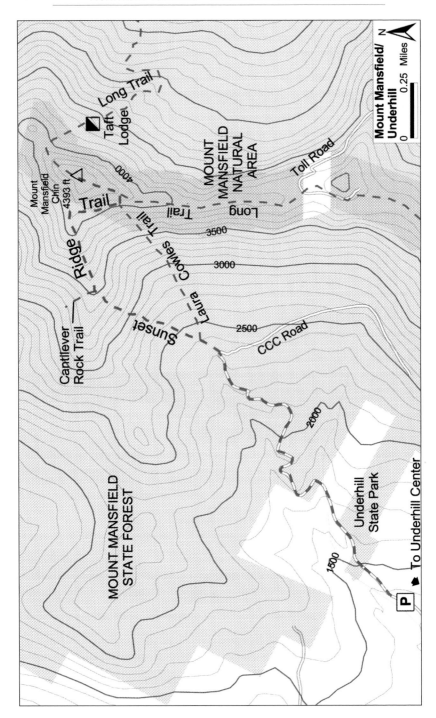

Mount Mansfield/
Underhill

N

0   0.25   Miles

Long Trail

Taft
Lodge

MOUNT
MANSFIELD
NATURAL
AREA

Toll Road

Mount
Mansfield
Chin
4393 ft

4000

Trail

Long Trail

Ridge

3500

Cowles Trail

3000

Cantilever
Rock Trail

Laura

Sunset

2500

CCC Road

2000

MOUNT MANSFIELD
STATE FOREST

Underhill
State Park

1500

To Underhill Center

P

⑳ Mount Mansfield

Location: Underhill
Distance: 3.7 mi.
Elevation Gain: 3,000 ft.

This hike to the summit of Vermont's highest peak is one of the premier snowshoe outings in the state. The trail passes through several vegetation zones, culminating in an above-treeline zone that can feel like the Arctic. Views stretch across three states (New York, New Hampshire and Vermont) and into the province of Quebec. This can be a difficult trip due to the potential for extreme weather, ice and deep snow on the trail and the 3000- ft. elevation gain. Depending on seasonal ice conditions, snowshoe crampons may not provide sufficient grip above treeline and it may be necessary to use either instep or full crampons. A word of caution: approximately one mile of this hike is above treeline and high winds can cause reduced visibility or whiteout conditions, making route finding nearly impossible.

GETTING THERE: From the three-way stop on Pleasant Valley Road in Underhill Center, continue north for 1 mi. to the road for Underhill State Park (signed). Turn right and continue 2 mi. to a plowed parking area along the road. The remainder of the road to the state park is not maintained in winter and it is foolish to attempt driving further.

DESCRIPTION: From the parking area (0.0 mi.), the route follows the unplowed State Park Road 0.75 mi. to the first gate. It winds left, then right for several hundred yards to the ranger station, campground (both closed in winter) and trailhead register. From here, the route follows an old CCC Road, constructed by the Civilian Conservation Corps in the 1930s, 1 mi. to the start of the Sunset Ridge Trail. It is also possible to slightly shorten the distance by taking the Eagle Cut Trail, which cuts off the switchbacks on the road. The Sunset Ridge trailhead is marked by a bulletin board, signpost and picnic table, making it a nice place to stop. From here, the route turns left to follow a narrow, wooded path. The trail crosses a bridge and reaches a junction with the Laura Cowles Trail (0.1 mi.), which offers an alternate route to the summit ridge. Although shorter and more direct, this trail is also steeper, viewless and often unbroken. It does, however, provide shelter from wind and weather up to almost the 4000-ft. level. The Sunset Ridge Trail crosses a series of small bridges as it begins to climb toward the ridge. At 0.7 mi. from the CCC Road, the Cantilever Rock spur trail enters on the left. This 0.1 mi. detour leads to a huge spear-like rock jutting out from the cliff, performing an improbable balancing act that looks as though it could end at any moment. The main trail continues its steady upward climb, finally attaining the open ridge 0.5 mi. from Cantilever Rock. Since the blue blazes are often snow-covered along the open ridge, the trail route is marked by rock cairns (piles of small rocks). From here, Sunset Ridge is a pure delight on a sunny winter day. This is a quintessential section of above-treeline trail with expansive views, delicate vegetation and a feeling of remoteness from the world below. The Champlain Valley and Adirondacks spread out to the west and Camels Hump rises above the rest of the Green Mountains to the south. Mt. Mansfield's Chin looms ahead and above. At 1.9 mi. from the CCC Road, just below the Chin, the trail turns sharply right and parallels the main ridge for 0.2 mi., passing the upper junction with the Laura Cowles Trail before intersecting the Long Trail on the ridge. The route now turns left to follow the white-blazed Long Trail to the Chin, the highest point in Vermont. On a clear day, it is possible to see the Presidential Range and Franconia Ridge in New Hampshire to the east, Lake Champlain and New York's Adirondack Mountains to the west and Jay Peak and the skyline of Montreal to the north. The deep gouge of Smugglers' Notch is below and northeast. Camels Hump is south and the Worcester Range southeast.

Snowshoeing near GMC headquarters, Waterbury Center, VT.

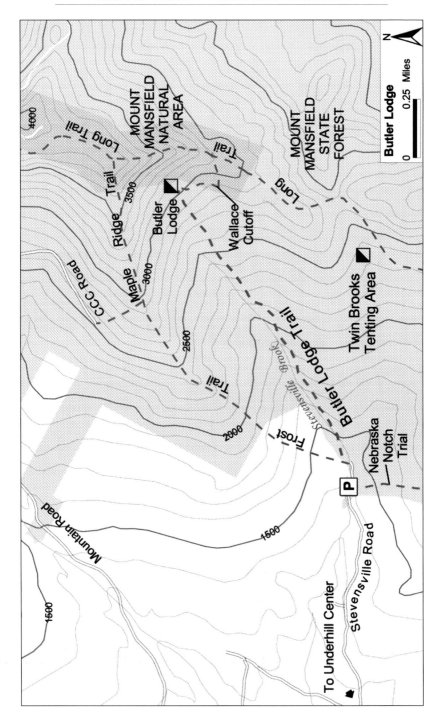

㉑ Butler Lodge

Location: Stevensville
Distance: 1.8 mi.
Elevation Gain: 1,560 ft.

The trail to Butler Lodge climbs steadily, although with no particularly steep sections, making it appropriate for hiking with both children and dogs. Because the hillside is easy to traverse, cross- country skiers also share the trail when snow conditions are good. From the porch at the lodge, Lake Champlain and the Adirondacks can be seen to the west and the cliffs below Mt. Mansfield's forehead loom above. Butler Lodge is an enclosed shelter, reconstructed by volunteers from the Burlington Section of the Green Mountain Club in 2000.

GETTING THERE: From Underhill Center, take Pleasant Valley Road for 0.2 mi. and turn right onto Stevensville Road. Pass the entrance to Maple Leaf Farm on the left at 1.1 mi. Just beyond the turn to Maple Leaf Farm, there is a small parking lot for cross-country skiers. Continue uphill on the often icy, narrow (one lane) road all the way to the end and the main parking lot, which is plowed in the winter. This is a popular area and on weekends the lot may be full. Additional parking is available in a few plowed turnouts along the road.

DESCRIPTION: From the signboard at the end of the main parking lot (0.0 mi.), the trail bears left onto a logging road, passing a cement and steel bridge on the left and continues through a gate. At 0.2 mi., a sign on a tree to the left marks the start of the Butler Lodge Trail. The trail enters the woods and almost immediately diverges right from a junction with the Frost Trail. It climbs gently at first, steepens through the mid-section, then levels near the lodge. The Wallace Cutoff, 100 ft. on the right before Butler Lodge, is a short connector, which leads 0.1 mi. to the Long Trail. It is possible to make a circuit snowshoe by taking the Long Trail south 2.6 mi. to the Nebraska Notch Trail, which descends 1.5 mi. back to the parking lot. From the front door of Butler Lodge, there is a commanding view of the Champlain Valley to the south and west. A better view to the south is on the trail just above the lodge, on the way to a junction with the Rock Garden Trail and the Wampahoofus Trail, which climbs steeply 0.8 mi. to The Forehead.

㉒ Nebraska Notch

Location: Stevensville
Distance: 2.2 mi.
Elevation Gain: 470 ft.

The Nebraska Notch Trail is an easy hike suitable for families, with choices to satisfy all tastes: a more difficult alternate trail for the last 0.4 mi., a bushwhack, beaver ponds and a sheltered destination. Because this is a popular trail, it is usually packed out. Dogs are permitted, but they must be kept under control as this trail is also used by skiers.

GETTING THERE: See directions for Butler Lodge.

DESCRIPTION: From the trailhead register at the end of the parking area (0.0 mi.), the Nebraska Notch Trail leaves right to climb gently to a beaver pond and bridge crossing at 1.4 mi. Just beyond the bridge, a narrow path leads down to the pond. If it is very cold and the ice is safe, it is shorter and easier to follow the edge of the pond rather than the trail. A short bushwhack upstream from the pond leads to a beautiful waterfall. From the bridge, the trail climbs a short hill and reaches the junction with the Long Trail at 1.5 mi. From here, it is possible to hike north on the Long Trail to Butler Lodge, then return to the parking area via the Butler Lodge Trail. The route to Taylor Lodge turns south (right) on the Long Trail. At first, it descends to the other end of the beaver pond, turns left, passes a smaller beaver pond and reaches the junction with the Clara Bow Trail at 1.8 mi. To the right, the Long Trail climbs moderately before descending rather steeply to Taylor Lodge (2.2 mi.). The lodge is about 100 ft. left at a sharp right-hand turn in the trail.

The Clara Bow Trail, once considered an alternate for the Long Trail, is a more difficult route. It was named for a silent movie star because "It is like her – beautiful but tough." Passing through Nebraska Notch, a deep cleft strewn with boulders, the trail is filled with rugged beauty: jumbled boulders and steep walls. At one point it goes into a cave under a rock and comes out the other end by a ladder. This can be challenging at any time, but especially when there is ice, which is frequently. Beyond the cave, the trail slabs a side hill until reaching Taylor Lodge.

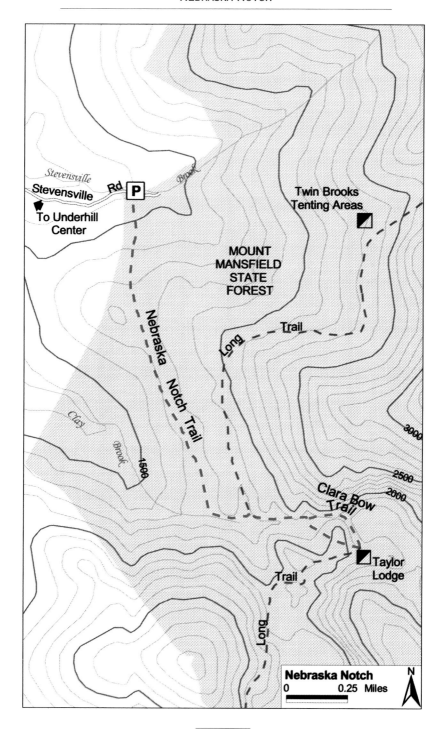

Stevensville

Stevensville Rd P Brook

Twin Brooks
Tenting Areas

To Underhill
Center

MOUNT
MANSFIELD
STATE
FOREST

Long Trail

Nebraska Notch Trail

Clay Brook

1500

3000

2500

2000

Clara Bow Trail

Taylor
Lodge

Trail

Long

Nebraska Notch
0   0.25   Miles

N

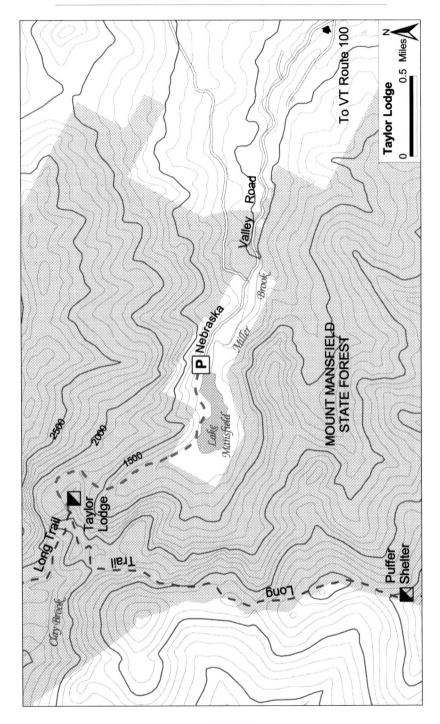

㉓ Taylor Lodge

Location: Stowe
Distance: 1.6 mi.
Elevation Gain: 650 ft.

This approach to Taylor Lodge passes the remains of the village of Mansfield and, in light snow years, abandoned cellar holes are visible from the trail. Nearby, a grove of towering white pines provides a majestic setting for the long-forgotten community. The current Taylor Lodge was built by the Burlington Section of the Green Mountain Club in 1978 and is named in honor of James P. Taylor, founder of the Long Trail

GETTING THERE: From Vt. 100, 2.5 mi. south of Stowe village, take the Moscow Road west toward the hamlet of Moscow. At 0.4 mi., bear left at the Y. At 2.0 mi., bear right onto Nebraska Valley Road. After the pavement ends at 4.0 mi., continue up Nebraska Valley Road until an intersection with County Road at 5.9 mi. Turn right onto County Road and take the first left into the winter parking area. The parking lot is plowed and there is usually space for 6-8 cars.

DESCRIPTION: A small sign at the edge of the clearing (west-northwest) indicates where a blue-blazed trail begins. At the end of the plowed road, the trail continues past the closed gate and onto the private road to the Trout Club, which is closed in winter. Just before the Trout Club lodge, it turns right into the summer parking area and the start of the Lake Mansfield Trail (0.0 miles). The Trout Club is private property and hikers should stay on the blue blazed trail. From the trailhead register, the trail skirts the Trout Club's buildings and follows the north shore of the lake for 0.5 mi. It is nearly level at first, but begins a gradual climb after crossing a small stream. Near the top of the rise, the trail takes a sharp right turn. Just past this turn, an alternate winter trail to Taylor Lodge begins on the left (1.1 miles). This is also the site of the abandoned village of Mansfield. The main trail continues to climb past the start of the alternate route and enters a small gorge. The trail is narrow at this point and may not be passable if conditions are icy. It climbs along the wall of the gorge, past the spring, which is the source of water for Taylor Lodge. The trail crosses a stream, which may be difficult to cross during snow melt, then climbs gently past a beaver meadow, with views of the north wall of Nebraska Notch, to Taylor Lodge at 1.6 mi. The Long Trail is 0.1 mi. beyond.

The beginning of the alternate winter route is marked by a faded blue blaze on a tree to the left and orange surveyor's tape on a tree further back. It does not get much use and may have to be broken after recent snowfall. It crosses a small stream and continues for 0.4 mi., climbing steeply at times. Taylor Lodge is visible on the rocky outcrop above and Lake Mansfield can be seen through the trees below. The trail winds its way up to Taylor Lodge and the Long Trail just beyond.

James Green checks a trail blaze that in summer is eye high, 1930.

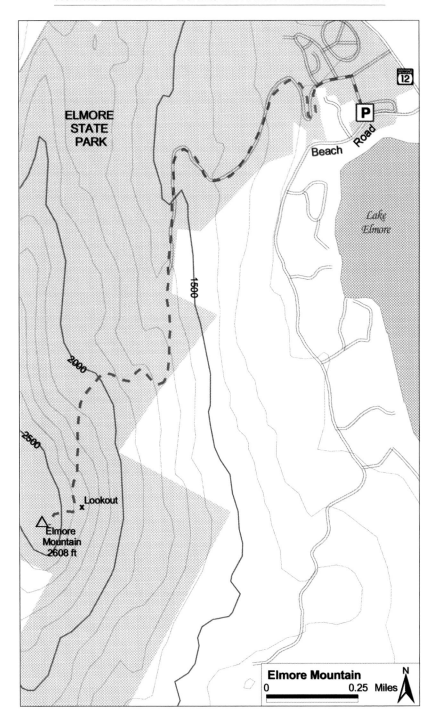

ELMORE
STATE
PARK

Beach Road

P

12

Lake
Elmore

1500

2000

2500

x Lookout

△
Elmore
Mountain
2608 ft

Elmore Mountain
0   0.25 Miles
N

㉔ Elmore Mountain

Location: Elmore
Distance: 1.9 mi.
Elevation Gain: 1,250 ft.

At 2,605 ft., Elmore Mountain is the lowest peak in the Worcester Range. Like the town, it was named for land grantee and early settler Colonel Samuel Elmore who hailed from Connecticut and served during the American Revolution. The winter trail follows the blue-blazed trail as it ascends moderately to a lookout plateau below the fire tower, where there are impressive views to the east.

GETTING THERE: Since Elmore State Park is closed in winter, the winter parking area is located at the beach parking lot. From Vt. 12 in Elmore at the north end of Lake Elmore, turn west on Beach Road. The plowed parking area is on the right, across from the beach house.

DESCRIPTION: The winter hiking route begins near the entrance to the parking area at a barrier (0.0 mi.). It passes to the left of the park's entrance booth and turns left onto the park road, which was built by the CCC (Civilian Conservation Corps), as were the shelters and fireplaces. After passing the camping area on the right, the road veers first left, then right, then left again before beginning a straighter course upward. Immediately beyond a picnic shelter on the right, it passes through an iron gate, continuing uphill to a height of land (1.0 mi.) where it narrows to a footpath. The Mt. Elmore Trail turns off to the right into the woods. The Catamount Trail, blazed with blue diamonds, continues straight. While this turn is well marked by a sign, "Elmore Mountain Trail," and by blue blazes, the blazes may be obscured by snow and unreliable as guides. At 1.9 mi., the trail reaches the lookout plateau, with a chimney marking the site of the former fire observer's cabin, which was burned by arson in 1983. From the clearing, there is a view down to Lake Elmore and Elmore village and another up to the right of the summit fire tower. While there is a trail that continues to the tower, it is steep and often icy, requiring the use of full crampons. This trail to the summit leaves to the right from the main trail, a short distance before the lookout.

㉕ Mount Worcester

Location: Worcester
Distance: 2.5 mi.
Elevation Gain: 1,970 ft.

The Worcester Range parallels the high ridge of the Green Mountains to the east and stretches from White Rocks Mtn. north of the Winooski River to Mt. Elmore south of the Lamoille River. Worcester Mtn., in the middle of the range, offers a steady climb to an open summit with wonderful views of both the Green Mountains to the west and the White Mountains in New Hampshire to the east.

GETTING THERE: From Vt. 12 in Worcester, follow Minister Brook Road 1.5 mi. west to Hampshire Hill Road. Turn right and ascend the hills to Hancock Brook Road (3.7 mi.). Turn left on Mountain Road and park in the barely plowed lane to the right just before the last house on the road.

DESCRIPTION: The route follows the lane around the last house to the summer parking lot (0.0 mi.), where it leaves the clearing past a trailhead register to follow a narrow woods road uphill in the valley of Hancock Brook. As the trail climbs up the valley, it leaves the stream and begins a series of steep ascents, which are made easier in winter by snow covering the rocky, uneven trail. At the top of the steep pitches (2.2 mi.), the trail enters the spruce-fir forest at the base of some open ledges. On a beautiful winter day, the ascent over the snow-covered ledges is a joy, with views at every pause, and snow smoothing the rough spots. From the summit (2.5 mi.), Mt. Hunger lies to the south, Camels Hump and Mt. Mansfield to the west, Elmore Mtn. to the north and the White Mountains to the east.

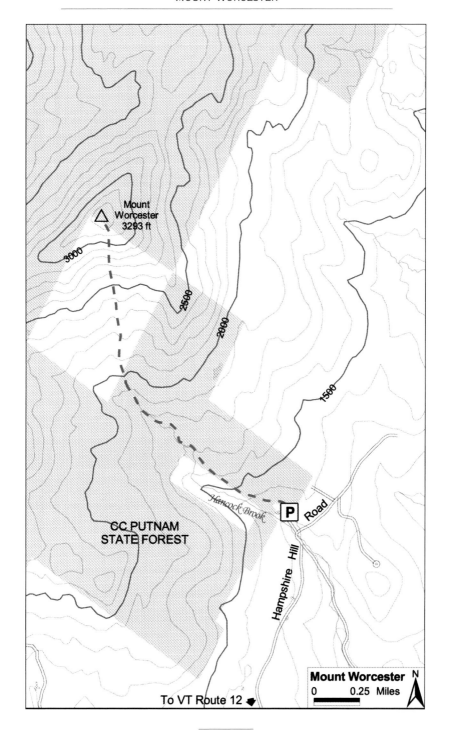

Mount Worcester
3293 ft

CC PUTNAM
STATE FOREST

Hancock Brook

P Road

Hampshire Hill

Mount Worcester N
0   0.25 Miles

To VT Route 12

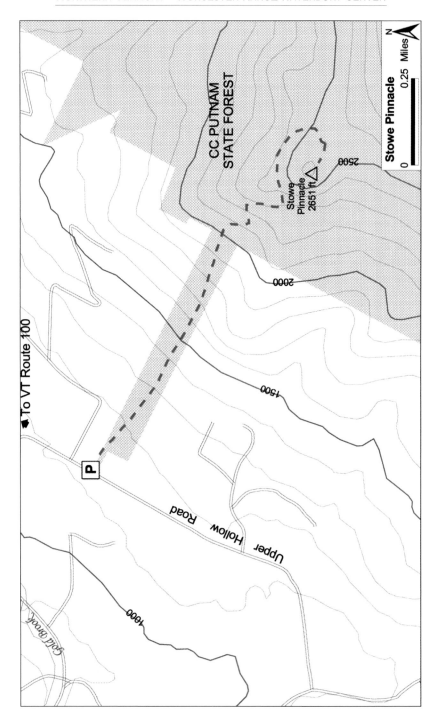

㉖ Stowe Pinnacle

Location: Stowe
Distance: 1.4 mi.
Elevation Gain: 1,520 ft.

Although nearly 800 ft. lower in elevation than nearby Mt. Hunger, this prominent spur on the northwest flank of Hogback Mtn. offers a dramatic view of the Stowe Valley and the Green Mountain ridgeline. From the open summit dome, the mountain panorama extends from Jay Peak in the north to Mts. Ethan and Ira Allen in the south, with Whiteface Mtn., Mt. Mansfield, Nebraska Notch, Bolton Mtn., and Camel's Hump in between. Much of the Worcester Range, including Hogback Mtn., can be seen to the southeast.

GETTING THERE: From Exit 10 of Interstate 89, turn north on Vt. 100 for 7.8 mi. Turn right on Gold Brook Road. After passing a bridge at 0.3 mi., veer left to continue on Gold Brook Road. At the junction with Upper Hollow Road at 1.6 mi., turn right and look for the parking lot on the left just past Pinnacle Road.

DESCRIPTION: The blue-blazed Stowe Pinnacle Trail leaves the back of the parking lot, through a tangle of overgrown pasture and a scattering of hawthorn and apple trees. The trail soon enters the forest near the trail register and passes by a large glacial erratic: a boulder left by retreating glaciers close to 10,000 years ago. The tall white pines mark the edges of fields and pastures once tended by area farmers. As the incline grows steeper a series of switchbacks lead through older hardwoods, where the vertical slashes of bear claws mark the gray bark of beech trees. The trail winds easily for almost 1.0 mi. to a pair of steep rock staircases, sometimes glazed with ice, leading to a junction just below the saddle. A vista a few steps to the northwest (left) gives a taste of the views to come. The trail now veers eastward (right) to approach the Pinnacle from behind. It dips briefly then ascends once again, slowly turning clockwise to enter a spruce-fir stand and a junction with the Hogback Trail to Skyline Ridge. The Pinnacle Trail bears east (right) and climbs through stunted evergreens to emerge on the rocky summit. The Green Mountains are directly ahead, with the Worcester Range behind and to the left. The large body of water in the foreground is Waterbury Reservoir.

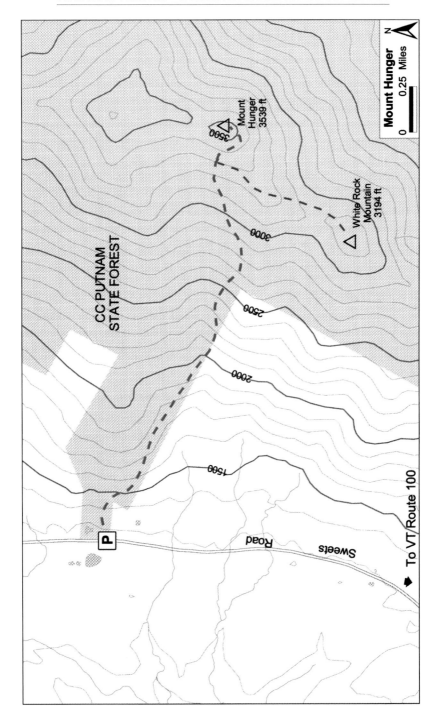

㉗ Mount Hunger

Location: Waterbury
Distance: 2.2 mi.
Elevation Gain: 2,290 ft.

The open summit of Mt. Hunger offers spectacular views of New Hampshire's White Mountains to the east and Vermont's Green Mountains to the west. Mt. Hunger is part of the Worcester Range, which rises from the Winooski River Valley and extends north to Elmore Mtn. Although the absence of trees on the summit is commonly attributed to a long-ago forest fire, the presence of rare alpine plant species suggests that climate may have played a role in depressing the treeline as well. The cliffs and ledges, laid bare by glaciers thousands of years ago, may never have supported more than a scattering of the stunted spruce and fir, known as krummholz or crooked wood, that hugs the windswept summit today.

GETTING THERE: From Exit 10 on Interstate 89, turn north on Vt. 100 toward Stowe to a traffic light. Continue through the light for 2.5 mi. to Howard Street on the right. If traveling south on Vt. 100 from Stowe, Howard Street is on the left 0.3 mi. south of the Cold Hollow Cider Mill. Follow Howard Street 0.3 mi. to a left turn on Maple Street, then a right turn onto Loomis Hill Road, just past the fire station. At the top of the hill, the road bears left and reaches a small parking area on the right at 3.8 mi. from Vt. 100.

DESCRIPTION: From the parking area (0.0 mi.), the blue-blazed Waterbury Trail to Mt. Hunger leads past the trailhead register into a hardwood forest. It jogs to the southeast and after a half mile, climbs a rock outcrop and steep incline to the east. It parallels a stream and waterfall for a short distance, crossing the stream at a level spot above the falls. The smooth rocks here are often icy, but the water is rarely too deep to cross safely. The trail turns sharply upslope as it nears the halfway point, then continues climbing via a series of switchbacks through birch and evergreen. It passes through a forest clearing and enters a forest of small, tightly-spaced spruce and fir where short scrambles indicate the summit is near. At 2.0 mi., the White Rocks Trail enters from the right and the main trail continues 0.2 mi. straight ahead up a last steep pitch to treeline. Even in winter, it is important to stay on the trail and avoid stepping on the alpine plants. Although they have adapted to arctic weather, they have not adapted to being stepped on. From the summit, the White Mountains of New Hampshire define the eastern horizon and the Adirondacks of New York State rise over Lake Champlain far to the west. A patchwork of snow-covered fields and forests stretches for miles in every direction. On a clear day, Vermont's 4,000 ft. summits form an unmatchable Green Mountain panorama: Killington Peak far to the south, Abraham, Ellen and Camel's Hump to the southwest, and Mansfield to the northwest. Two other blue-blazed trails leave the summit: the Middlesex Trail descends the eastern slope along the route of a 19th century carriage road and the Skyline Trail traverses the ridgeline north to Mt. Worcester.

Snowshoeing on the Waterbury Trail to the top of Mount Hunger.

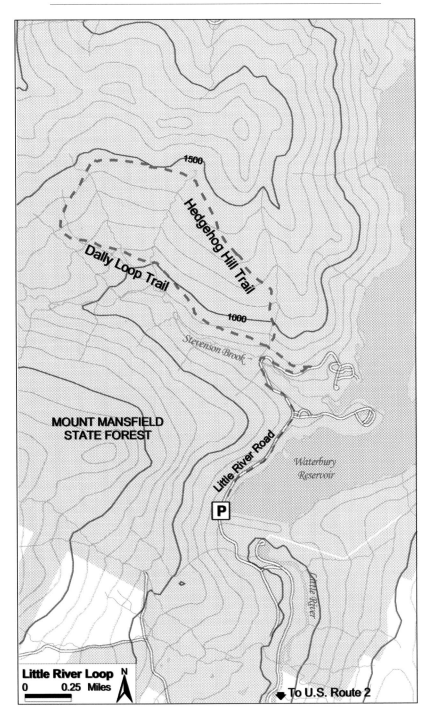

Little River Loop

0   0.25 Miles

N

To U.S. Route 2

28 Little River Loop

Location: Waterbury
Distance: 6.4 mi.
Elevation Gain: 650 ft.

Little River State Park lies in the southwest corner of the 40,000-acre Mt. Mansfield State Forest. The park's earthen Waterbury Dam was completed in 1938 by the Civilian Conservation Corps after the serious flood of 1927. The hike route follows old roads past the remains of stone walls, family cemeteries, forgotten foundations and an abandoned house. Part of it is on snowmobile trail, which can be a welcome relief from breaking trail in deep snow.

GETTING THERE: From U.S. 2, 1.5 mi. west of Vt. 100 in Waterbury, follow Little River Road north 2.7 mi. to the Waterbury Dam. Park near the dam's western abutment, so as not to block any plowed road. If the hill leading to the top of the dam is icy, there is limited parking at the bottom in front of a closed gate. Again, vehicles should be parked so as not to block the gate or the plowed road.

DESCRIPTION: From the top of the dam, the route begins on the un-plowed, but usually packed out, road leading uphill to the campground contact station (0.6 mi.) where it bears left and continues past the campground to the first right. It descends to Stevenson Brook, crossing it on a bridge, then follows the road uphill and around a corner to the Nature Trail and History Hike bulletin board (1.3 mi.). The route turns sharply left and climbs to a junction with the Hedgehog Hill Trail, an old road, on the right. Turning right on the more lightly used and often unbroken Hedgehog Hill Trail, the trail steadily ascends through birch forest. On the left at 2.0 mi., it passes the Ricker Family Cemetery, framed by cedar tree plantings in the midst of northern hardwood forest. Beyond the cemetery, the trail levels, reaching a snowmobile trail and turning left to follow the hard-packed route (2.8 mi.). The trail descends gradually to Ricker Corners (3.1 mi.), where the hiking trail turns left to the leave the snowmobile trail and follow the Dalley Loop Trail downhill past the Goodell Place, the last remaining building on the History Hike Loop. The gentle descent continues to the junction with the Hedgehog Hill Trail (on the left), where the hike retraces the route back to the dam.

Central Vermont

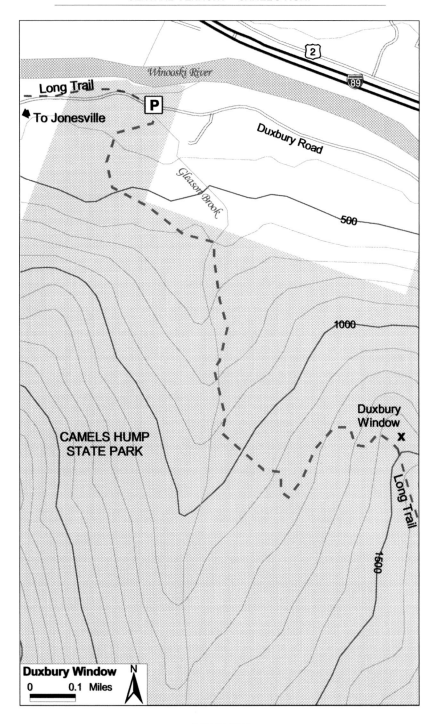

29 Duxbury Window

Location: Jonesville
Distance: 1.6 mi.
Elevation Gain: 800 ft.

This hike on the Long Trail begins at the trailhead on Duxbury Road near the Winooski River, the lowest point on the Long Trail. It follows Bamforth Ridge, one of the flanks of Camel's Hump, which was named for tireless trail worker, Eugene L. Bamforth (1895-1970). Duxbury Window is the first lookout on the ridge. Since the trail is popular, it is likely to be already packed by previous snowshoers.

GETTING THERE: From U.S. 2 in Jonesville at Cochran Road, cross the bridge over the Winooski River and turn left on Duxbury Road, also called River Road. Continue 3.1 mi. to the plowed parking lot on the right where there is a prominent Long Trail sign at the entrance. From Waterbury, take Exit 10 from Interstate 89, turn right (south) on Vt. 100, then left on U.S. 2 at the bottom of the grade. Turn right on Winooski Street to cross the river, then right on River Road and follow it 6.0 mi. to the parking lot on the left.

DESCRIPTION: The white-blazed Long Trail leaves from the back of the parking lot where there is a trail register (0.0 mi.). It climbs gradually, then descends briefly to Gleason Brook (0.6 mi.), a tributary of the Winooski, which it crosses on a sturdy foot bridge built by volunteers in 1994. The trail ascends again, turning right on an old logging road high above the brook. It turns left away from the brook and climbs steadily via a series of switchbacks through hardwood forest where there are changing views of the surrounding hills. It is possible to hear the faint din of traffic from the interstate. The trail then steepens just before reaching Duxbury Window (1.6 mi.). The Green Mountain Club has installed a rustic bench here, although it may be buried under deep snow. The view from the "window" is framed by the Winooski Valley and Bolton Mtn. rising on the other side of the valley. The Long Trail beyond the Window leads via "banister ledge" to a rocky outcropping known as Spruce Knob. However, this section of trail is steep and often icy, no longer an easy to moderate climb.

㉚ Camel's Hump

Location: Huntington
Distance: 2.4 mi.
Elevation Gain: 2,461 ft.

The Burrows Trail offers the easiest access to the summit of Camel's Hump and its spectacular view of the Champlain Valley and Adirondacks, as well as the major peaks of the Green Mountains. Although the trail is not particularly steep, it does climb persistently to the Hut Clearing. While there is considerable elevation gain from the parking lot to the summit, the trail is popular and, therefore, usually well-packed by both snowshoers and skiers.

GETTING THERE: From Huntington Center (not to be confused with Huntington village, which is 2.5 mi. north), turn east onto Camel's Hump Road and follow it 2.8 mi. to the end where there is a large plowed parking lot. This is a popular trailhead in winter and the lot often fills. There is limited parking for six vehicles 0.7 mi. back down the road at the start of the Forest City Trail.

DESCRIPTION: The blue-blazed trail leaves the far end of the parking area (0.0 mi.), passing a trailhead register and the Burrows-Forest City Connector on the right. It climbs gradually, but steadily through mixed hardwoods in an area internationally recognized as a research site for forest health, especially acid deposition. The trail crosses several small streams as it ascends, sometimes steeply, through spruce-fir forest to the ridge between Camel's Hump and nearby Bald Hill (1.5 mi.). It then levels somewhat until reaching the junction with the Long Trail at the Hut Clearing (2.1 mi.), where there is still a clearing but no longer a hut. This sheltered spot is often used by hikers to don additional clothing for the climb above treeline to the summit. The Long Trail north over Bamforth Ridge leaves on the left and the Monroe Trail to Duxbury is straight ahead. From the clearing, the route now follows the Long Trail south (right) 0.3 mi. steeply up over open rock to the summit.

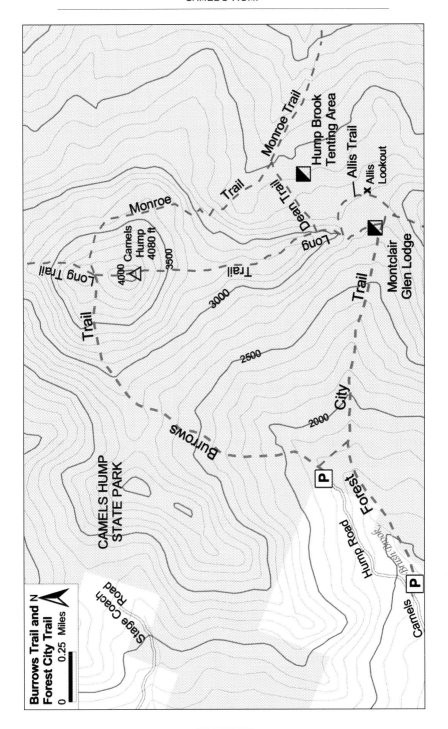

Burrows Trail and
Forest City Trail

N

0   0.25   Miles

CAMELS HUMP
STATE PARK

Stage Coach
Road

Hump Road

Bristol Brook

Camels

Montclair
Glen Lodge

Long   City

Forest

Trail

Burrows

Trail

2000

2500

3000

3500

4000

Camels
Hump
4080 ft

Long Trail

Trail

Monroe

Trail

Monroe Trail

Dean Trail

Long

Trail

Allis Trail

Allis
Lookout

Hump Brook
Tenting Area

A view of Camel's Hump from the south.

㉛ Forest City Trail

Location: Huntington
Distance: 2.2 mi.
Elevation Gain: 1,706 ft.

This less often used trail on the west side of Camel's Hump offers an opportunity for solitude on one of Vermont's most popular mountains. It begins by passing through the historic remnants of a logging camp, crosses numerous frozen streams and ends at the site of the original 1917 Montclair Glen Lodge on the Long Trail. From there, it is possible to finish the climb to the summit of Camel's Hump or have lunch with a view on the Allis Trail.

GETTING THERE: See driving directions for the Burrows Trail to Camel's Hump and park at the turnout 0.7 mi. from the parking lot at the end of Camel's Hump Road.

DESCRIPTION: From Camel's Hump Road (0.0 mi.), the blue-blazed Forest City Trail begins on an old woods road, then turns right away from the road, crosses Brush Brook and enters the abandoned Forest City Civilian Conservation Corps camp built in the 1930s, where there are the remains of a furnace. This marks the boundary of Camel's Hump State Park. The trail now follows another woods road, crosses Brush Brook again and climbs to a junction with the Forest City Connector, which leaves left to end at the Burrows Trail. From the Forest City Connector, the trail bears right, leaving the logging roads behind, and climbs gradually to its junction with the Long Trail (2.2 mi.), 200 ft. north of the current Montclair Glen Lodge. From here, it is 1.9 mi. north on the Long Trail to the summit of Camel's Hump and 1.0 mi. south to Mt. Ethan Allen. Shorter options include: 0.3 mi. north to Wind Gap or 0.2 mi. south to the Allis Trail, both of which offer dramatic views of Camel's Hump.

PLEASE REFER TO THE MAP ON PAGE 77

32 Peacham Bog

Location: Groton
Distance: 2.6 mi.
Elevation Gain: 400 ft.

Peacham Bog, located in Groton State Forest, offers an easy snowshoe hike for beginners and families. The trail passes through forest of balsam fir and red spruce, eventually leading to open views of the bog and surrounding mountains. The winter bog is a perfect place to look for signs of wildlife such as moose and fisher.

GETTING THERE: From US 302 in Groton, turn north onto Vt. 232 (across from Groton Gas Station and Diner) toward Groton State Forest. Travel 5.3 mi., turn right on Boulder Beach Road and follow it 1.6 mi. to the Nature Center. Turn left into the Nature Center where there is ample winter parking. Alternatively, from US 2 in Marshfield, turn south on Vt. 232 and follow it 8.3 mi. to Boulder Beach Road on the left.

DESCRIPTION: The blue-blazed Peacham Bog Trail leaves the large parking lot from the northeast corner, opposite the Visitor Center (0.0 mi.). The trailhead sign may be buried in snow, but it is located at the edge of the woods. The trail climbs a short embankment and enters the woods before quickly leveling. The remainder of the hike is on level terrain through a mixed hardwood forest and does not gain any significant elevation. The trail crosses the Coldwater Brook Trail at 0.2 mi. and a small brook on a bridge at 0.4 mi. At 0.7 mi., it turns right onto a woods road, then immediately left back into the woods. The trail is not signed at this junction. From here it ascends gently through woods and around interesting boulders. The trail crosses a small stream, entering the Peacham Bog Natural Area at 2.0 mi. Here, there is a sign reminding hikers to stay on the trail, given the sensitive and fragile nature of the bog. The bog is the second largest peat bog (peat moss) in Vermont, one of the two "raised" bogs in the state. The trail in the vicinity of the bog is level as it skirts around the southern side and meets the Martin's Pond Trail at 2.6 mi. The trail continues through the open bog to a viewing bench on the southwestern end. From the bench, there are sweeping views of the bog itself as well as of the surrounding mountains in Groton State Forest.

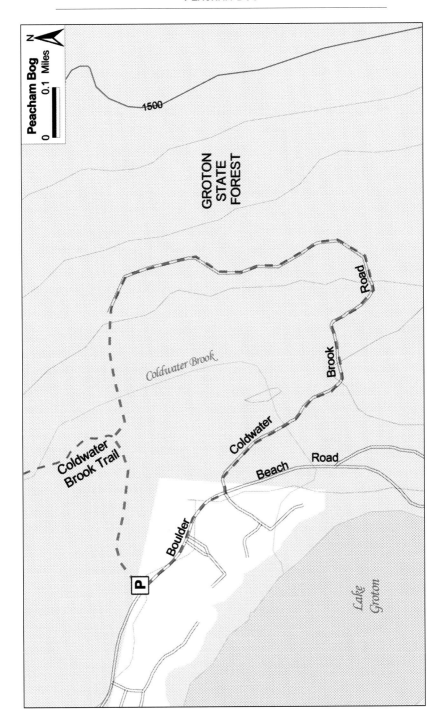

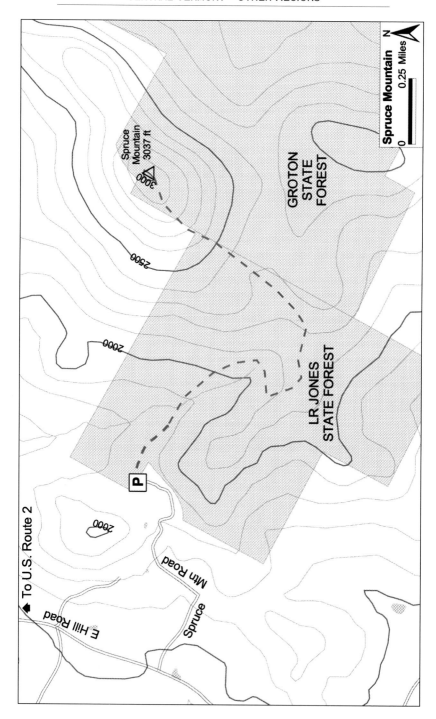

㉝ Spruce Mountain

Location: Plainfield
Distance: 2.2 mi.
Elevation Gain: 1,180 ft.

Although Spruce Mtn. was first established as a fire lookout in 1919, the current tower originally stood atop Bellevue Hill in St. Albans and was moved in 1943-44. The summit has sweeping views to the southeast and plenty of room for a winter picnic. Snowshoes with crampons are strongly recommended for the steep last half mile. Full crampons or creepers may be necessary.

GETTING THERE: From Plainfield, travel 0.4 mi. east on Main Street to East Hill Road. Turn right on East Hill Road and follow it 3.8 mi. to Spruce Mtn. Road. Turn left on Spruce Mtn. Road for 0.3 mi. and turn left again (no sign). The trailhead is 0.7 mi. farther at the end of the dirt road where there is a large parking area.

From East Barre, follow Vt. 302 east 1.1 mi. from the junction with Vt. 110 and turn north on Reservoir Road. Continue 5.6 mi. to a right turn on East Hill Road (pavement ends at 4.9 mi.), then turn right again on Spruce Mtn. Road.

DESCRIPTION: The unblazed, but well-traveled, trail leaves the parking area (0.0 mi.) to follow an old road past a state signboard and climb gently through mixed hardwoods and softwoods for 1 mi. After passing through a large clearing, it narrows into a footpath, enters the woods and begins to rise more steeply through softwoods and birch. At 1.5 mi., an intriguing rock formation on the right side of the trail is worthy of exploration into the cave-like structures. Beyond these rocks, the trail steepens and is often icy. The summit is reached at 2.0 mi., where there are still remains of the fire warden's cabin. The fire tower, which was repaired in 2004-2005, is in good condition, however, the steps tend to be icy.

34 Paine Mountain

Location: Northfield
Distance: 2.9 mi.
Elevation Gain: 1,650 ft.

Paine Mtn. is a central Vermont recreational area easily accessible from Interstate 89. According to a guidebook by Northfield resident William E. Osgood, the mountain is crisscrossed by a network of gravel roads, some of which date back to when Northfield was settled in 1784. Norwich University owns much of the land on Paine Mountain and welcomes hikers. The summit is forested with limited views of Berlin Pond, the Barre/Montpelier area and the Worcester Range through the bare trees. Northfield village may also be seen from open meadows along the trail.

GETTING THERE: From Exit 5 of Interstate 89, follow Vt. 64 West down the hill. At the bottom (2.9 mi.), turn right on Vt. 12 North toward Northfield. At 4.4 mi., a white-fenced area with a gazebo and the Norwich University Visitors Center sign is on the right. The Plumley Armory is on the left. Just beyond this point, after the intersection with Spring Street, parking is available on the right side of the street. On weekends, it may be possible to park in the lot near the armory or at the visitors center.

DESCRIPTION: From the parking area, the route follows Crescent Avenue toward the gazebo. The gated entrance to the former Norwich University ski area is just past the gazebo on the left (0.0 mi.), with the brown base lodge building 500 ft. back from the street. The route passes the former lodge and continues up the cleared ski slope to a well-used trail that enters the woods on the left. At a four-way junction (0.25 mi.), the trail continues straight, up the hill and around a gate. It passes a series of mounds topped by cupolas: water storage for the village. It then sweeps right (0.5 mi.) and continues uphill through an open field with views of the mountains surrounding Northfield. The trail reenters the woods and reaches a fork at 0.9 mi., marked by a strip of white cloth tied to a tree. Bearing right, it continues uphill. The trail passes a beaver pond (1.6 mi.) and comes to a T-junction. It turns right and climbs moderately. As it nears the summit, the trail levels and makes a sharp left turn (2.5 mi.). From here, it is another 0.4 mi. on easy grades to the summit. Continuing straight at the sharp left turn (2.5 mi.) leads to an open area with a shelter.

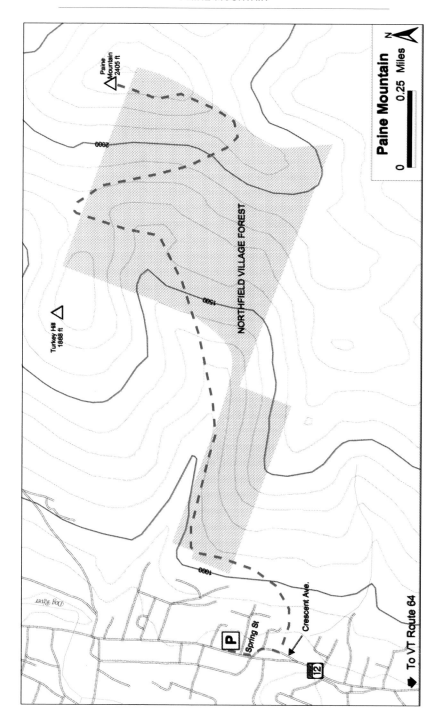

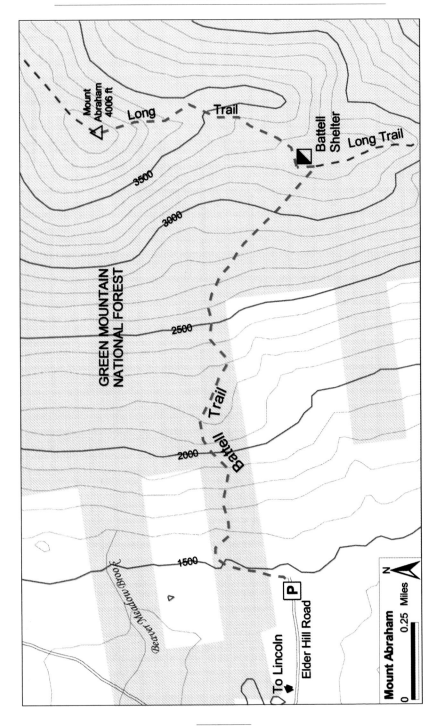

㉟ Mount Abraham

Location: Lincoln
Distance: 2.9 mi.
Elevation Gain: 2,500 ft.

Mt. Abraham sits at the southern end of Mt. Lincoln between Appalachian and Lincoln Gaps. At just over 4,000 ft., its alpine summit supports a colony of rare mountain vegetation, usually covered in winter by layers of rime and windblown snow. Except for a short scramble up the granite face just below the summit, this is a moderate, pleasant snowshoe hike and, because of its popularity, the trail is often well-packed and easy to follow.

GETTING THERE: From Main Street in Lincoln by the general store, turn north on Quaker Street. At 0.7 mi. turn right onto U.S. Forest Service Road 350, also known as Elder Hill Road, where a sign at the intersection points to the Battell Trail. Continue on Elder Hill Road 1.9 mi. to a gradual left turn, past a farm on the right. The trailhead is 0.1 mi. from the turn, although this final stretch is not maintained in winter. There is limited parking at the left turn and hikers should pull off the road to avoid blocking driveways, other forest roads or the snowmobile right-of-way.

DESCRIPTION: From the signed trailhead (0.0 mi.), the blue-blazed Battell Trail climbs steadily eastward through maple and birch as it works its way along the side hill to the ridge. Generally, it follows the contour, angling across the fall line. At 1.0 mi., the trail bears uphill to the right and crosses two streams, the first on a puncheon-type, usually ice-covered, bridge. It broadens as it approaches the ridge and the junction with the white-blazed Long Trail (2.0 mi.). Turning left, the route to the summit now follows the Long Trail to Battell Shelter, a three-sided shelter built in 1967 by volunteers from the Farm and Wilderness Camp, and turns sharply left to pass the shelter's privy. The trail now climbs moderately through spruce-fir forest, gradually steepening as it nears the base of the ledges. Depending on snow and ice conditions, crampons may be more appropriate than snowshoes for the remainder of the climb to the summit. A wide rock enclosure marks the top of Mt. Abraham (2.9 mi.) from which there are possible views as far as Mt. Marcy, highest point in the Adirondacks, to the west, Killington Peak to the south and Belvidere Mtn. to the north.

36 Skylight Pond

Location: Ripton
Distance: 3.5 mi.
Elevation Gain: 1,650 ft.

A delightful summer hike, the Skylight Pond Trail is perhaps even better in winter. While masses of hikers descend on the justifiably popular Camel's Hump to the north, the Skylight Pond Trail is likely to be deserted. It has a quiet remote atmosphere, a welcome change from some of the busier winter hiking destinations.

GETTING THERE: From the center of Ripton, follow U. S. Forest Service Road 59, also known as the Natural Turnpike, for approximately 4.0 mi. to a usually well-maintained and spacious parking lot. Beyond this point, the road is closed from December 15 until the surface firms after the spring thaw.

DESCRIPTION: The route passes through the winter gate (0.0 mi.) and follows the fairly flat Forest Service road through hardwood forest. This road is also a well-packed snowmobile trail for the first mile. At Stream Mill Clearing and the summer parking lot on the left, the now blue-blazed trail departs from the right near the entrance to the lot. Initially, it passes through mixed hardwoods of maple, beech and yellow birch. Several logging roads cross the trail and care should be taken to follow the blazes. From the boundary of the Bread Loaf Wilderness Area (1.4 mi.), the trail climbs gradually, but steadily at first, then ascends a series of switchbacks about 1.0 mi. from Stream Mill Clearing. Here the forest is increasingly made up of spruce and hemlock. After a final steep pitch, the top of the ridge and a signed junction with the Long Trail are reached just north of the summit of Battell Mtn. (3.4 mi.). Straight ahead is the spur trail to Skylight Pond. This gorgeous high-elevation pond will be a smooth expanse of snow and ice, but the setting is lovely all the same. On a hillside above the pond sits Skyline Lodge, a shelter built by the Green Mountain Club and U.S. Forest Service in 1987. It provides a fine place for lunch and a rest before the return hike.

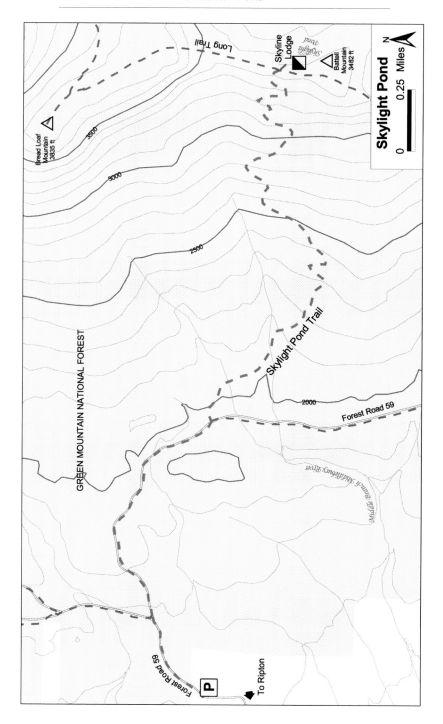

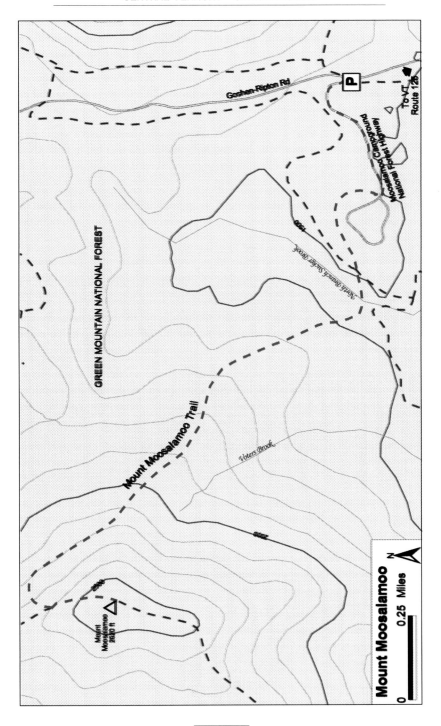

Mount Moosalamoo

㊲ Mount Moosalamoo

Location: Goshen
Distance: 2.7 mi.
Elevation Gain: 800 ft.

Moosalamoo is an Abenaki word meaning moose call. Located on the western edge of the Green Mountain National Forest between Middlebury and Brandon, Mt. Moosalamoo is a delightful mountain for snowshoeing with its gentle slopes and open woods, which make for an exhilarating descending glissade. The Moosalamoo Trail was constructed by the Youth Conservation Corps in 1975. A good resource for other trails in the region is found at moosalamoo.com.

GETTING THERE: From US 7 south of Middlebury, turn east on Vt. 125 for 5.2 mi., then right on Goshen Road (gravel). Follow this 3.3 mi. to the National Forest's Moosalamoo Campground on the right. As the campground and road are closed in winter, parking is on the side of Goshen Road near the entrance.

DESCRIPTION: The route follows the campground road past the entrance (0.0 mi.) to a sign for the Mt. Moosalamoo (right) and North Branch (left) Trails (0.4 mi.). The Mt. Moosalamoo Trail begins through the summer parking lot at a signboard where a good map of the area is posted. From here, the blue-blazed trail enters the woods and passes a small wooden sign on the left indicating the parking area and a shortcut to the campground. At 0.25 mi., it comes to a T-junction with a woods road blazed with blue diamonds. A small wooden sign indicates the trail turns right to follow the road for 50 yds., then turns sharply left, at another small sign, and descends to cross the North Branch of Voter Brook on a wooden footbridge (0.5 mi.). The trail now climbs gently, but steadily through open hardwoods. Just when it seems it will bypass the mountain altogether, it turns sharply left (not well-marked) to slab the hillside toward the ridge. At 2.0 mi., it passes a signed junction with the Oak Ridge Trail. The Mt. Moosalamoo Trail continues straight along the ridge another 0.3 mi. to a sign indicating vistas to the left and right. The signed wooded summit of Moosalamoo (2640') is 50 yds. to the left. There is a limited view to the east about 100 yds. beyond the summit. At the trail junction, the Oak Ridge Trail leads 0.15 mi. to an open ledge view east.

㊳ Baldtop Mountain

Location: Fairlee
Distance: 3.3 mi.
Elevation Gain: 1375 ft.

This appropriately named mountain offers sweeping views in all directions, but especially to the east and northeast, where the flat-topped summit of Mt. Cube and the summit of Mt. Moosilauke can be seen. The trail is part of the Cross Rivendell Trail, which, when completed, will link the towns of Vershire, West Fairlee, Fairlee and Orford. It is maintained by the Rivendell Trails Association.

GETTING THERE: From Interstate 91, take Exit 15 in Fairlee and turn west on Lake Morey Westside Road. Trailhead parking is at the Lake Morey boat ramp approximately 1.4 mi. from the Interstate.

DESCRIPTION: The trail begins across the road at a signboard (0.0 mi.), following light blue blazes as it climbs moderately via a switchback. At the top of the gravel pit, the Glen Falls Trail enters on the left (0.3 mi.). The trail now passes above the Glen Falls Gorge and intersects with the Echo Mtn. Trail (0.5 mi.) and Howdy's Trail (0.7 mi.). It bears right on the Bald Top Road (0.9 mi.), then left onto a woods road after passing the Cross Mountain Trail (1.1 mi.). A private driveway continues straight ahead. At the crest of the ridge, the trail passes a viewpoint, crosses a woods road (1.6 mi.) and traverses an area devastated by the 1938 hurricane as it switchbacks to the top of the ridge (2.3 mi.). The Bald Top Trail now bears right on a woods road and follows the ridge, turning right at two intersections to reach the summit clearing, where the views are spectacular in all directions. To the east lie the mountains of New Hampshire: the Smarts, Mt. Cube and Mt. Moosilauke.

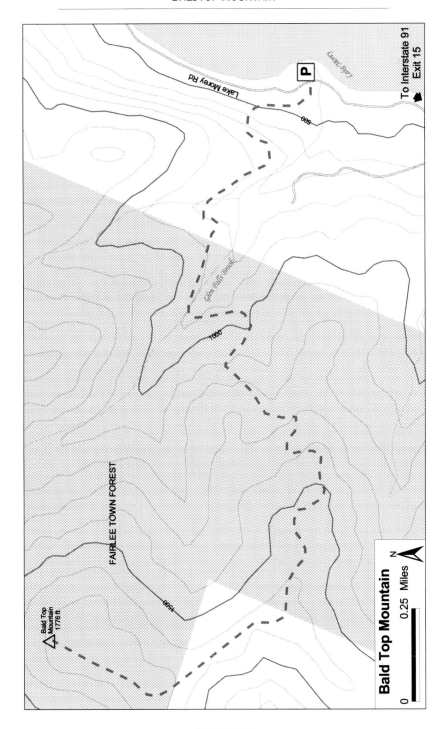

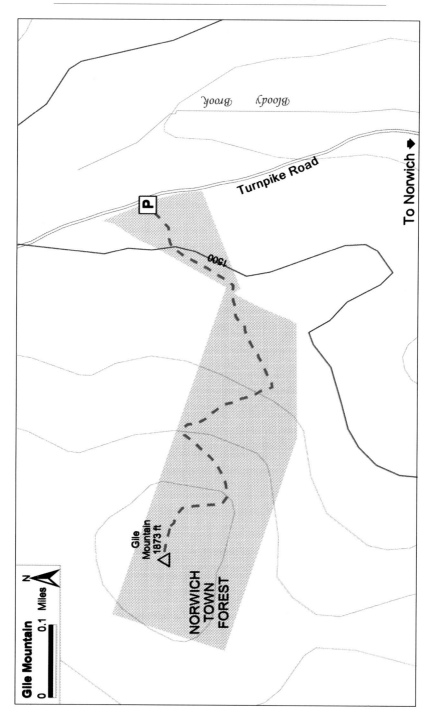

㊴ Gile Mountain

Location: Norwich
Distance: 0.7 mi.
Elevation Gain: 413 ft.

This is a short and not especially intense snowshoe with a grand payoff: a fire tower with commanding views of the Connecticut River Valley, Mts. Ascutney and Cardigan and long views to Killington, Camel's Hump and even a glimpse of the White Mountains. This is a dog friendly and child friendly route on town-owned property. It is a popular local hike in every season of the year, so unless it just snowed, the route will most likely be tracked out. The trail is maintained by the Trails Committee of the Norwich Conservation Commission.

GETTING THERE: From Exit 13 off Interstate 91, turn north on Vt. 5 to Norwich's Main Street. Pass the town green on the right, then the general store, Dan & Whit's, on the left. Continue 0.6 mi. past Dan & Whit's and turn left on Turnpike Road. At 0.9 mi. from the turn, stay left on Turnpike. The road will eventually change to gravel, then narrow and start to climb. At 5.2 mi. from the start of Turnpike, a Gile Mtn. parking sign is on the right and the small parking lot on the left, which is plowed in winter.

DESCRIPTION: The blue-blazed trail climbs gently from the parking lot (0.0 mi.) and makes a soft left onto an old flat woods road. At 0.15 mi., it turns right, leaving the woods road and ascending slightly. At 0.3 mi., the ski/bike trail leaves the hiking trail and veers left. The hiking trail continues straight ahead under the power line carrying electricity from the Wilder Dam. It crosses the cleared right of way and passes an intersection with the ski/bike trail just before entering the woods again, where it veers right to start the climb to the tower. After two meandering switchbacks, the trail turns right at 0.6 mi. to ascend the summit ridge. Ahead is a three-sided structure, the remains of the fire observer's cabin. Skirting it to the left, the trail continues to the tower, now visible ahead on the left. The tower was recently repaired and is in solid shape. However, even if the air is calm at the base, it will be colder and much windier at the top.

Note: At several points along the ascent, a second trail crosses the main trail. This is a cross-country ski and mountain bike trail designed by

Thetford ski trail designer John Morton. It leads, via a less direct route on longer switchbacks, to the tower and is marked by small signs that say "To Tower." Descending, this trail eventually leads to the power line right of way somewhat above the main trail. Following the power line down to the intersection with the hiking trail and turning left onto the hiking trail leads back to the parking lot.

Hikers checking out the cabin that stands at the top of Gile Mountain.

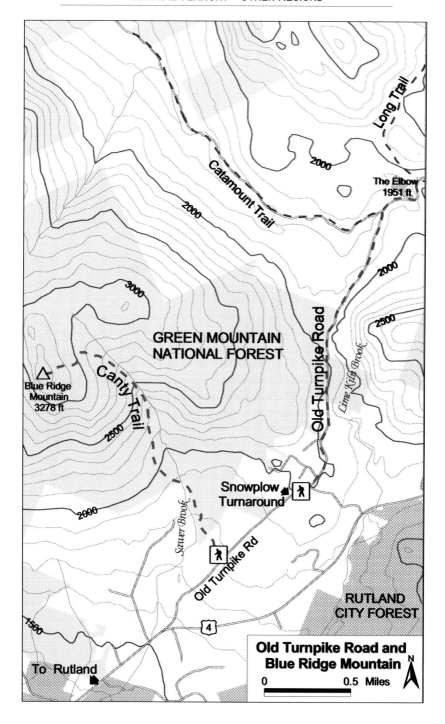

Long Trail

Catamount Trail

2000

The Elbow
1951 ft

2000

2000

3000

2500

GREEN MOUNTAIN
NATIONAL FOREST

Old Turnpike Road

Lime Kiln Brook

Blue Ridge
Mountain
3278 ft

Canty Trail

2500

Sauer Brook

2000

Snowplow
Turnaround

Old Turnpike Rd

1500

RUTLAND
CITY FOREST

4

To Rutland

**Old Turnpike Road and
Blue Ridge Mountain**

0   0.5 Miles

N

40 Blue Ridge Mountain

Location: Mendon
Distance: 2.4 mi
Elevation Change: 1,490 ft.

Because the Canty Trail rises more than 1,400 ft. in the last 1.6 mi., it is usually snowshoed only as far as the cascade on Sawyer Brook. Deep snow on the upper part of the trail can also be a problem for dogs. The trail is maintained by volunteers from the Killington Section of the Green Mountain Club and much treadway improvement was done by the Vermont Youth Conservation Corps in the summers of 2004 and 2005.

GETTING THERE: See driving and parking directions for Old Turnpike Road on page 101. The trailhead is 0.7 mi. from U.S. 4 on Old Turnpike Road and marked by a small "Blue Ridge" sign. Parking here is only legal when all four wheels are off the pavement, nearly impossible in winter unless you have a shovel to dig a hole in the snowbank for a car, and the local police are watchful.

Description: From Old Turnpike Road (0.0 mi), the blue-blazed Canty Trail passes around the gate and follows a wide lane. In 0.1 mi. it tends right, past the derelict buildings of Tall Timbers Camp. It enters a deciduous forest (0.2 mi), dipping down into a small ravine where a brook runs in warm months. The trail climbs steeply up the north bank and, entering the Green Mountain National Forest, descends the low ridge and joins a woods road. Continuing without elevation gain or loss for another 0.3 mi., the trail then dips downward, crosses sizeable Sawyer Brook (0.8 mi.) and climbs steeply up the opposite bank. It parallels the western side of this brook for 1.0 mi., first following a logging road through recently logged woods on both sides. From this point, following the Canty Trail can be a challenge if it has not been packed down. There is a network of logging roads that depart heading toward wood lots to the north and west and care must be taken to follow the blazes and remain near the brook. Thanks to the bare branches of winter, the Coolidge Range begins to appear. The trail ascends rather gradually until at 1.4 mi. it begins a steady climb. At 1.6 mi., it passes a spur trail, marked by a small sign, leading 100 ft. to the brook's largest cascade. It then trends west and departs the brook at 1.7 mi., entering a mixed hardwood/evergreen forest. At 2.1 mi., the woods road peters out and the Canty Trail turns left. It climbs steeply for 0.3 mi., passing a few mature hardwood trees before entering a stand of paper birch (2.4 mi.), just south of the summit. There are two viewpoints atop Blue Mtn. The first, at the summit, offers a hundred-mile view to the northeast of Spruce Mtn. and the other peaks of Groton State Forest. To the east is the Connecticut River Valley and Mt. Cube and Smarts Mtn. in New Hampshire. Continuing 20 yds. on the spur to Rutland Lookout, there is a view south down the Valley of Vermont to the Taconics, west to the Adirondacks, Bird Peak, Mt. Equinox, Dorset Peak, and Grandpa's Knob and east to the beautiful expanse of the Coolidge Range and the southern Green Mountains.

㊶ Old Turnpike Road

Location: Mendon
Distance: 1.4 mi.
Elevation Gain: 100 ft.

The Old Turnpike Road was once the Rutland-Stockbridge Turnpike, opened in the early 1800s. Before the road over 2,150-ft. Sherburne Pass was completed, the Turnpike was the main route over the mountains from Mendon to North Sherburne. It crosses the Green Mountains at The Elbow (1,951 ft.) where it makes a dogleg. Especially on the east side of the range, it is known as the Elbow Road and is popular with snowmobilers, cross-country skiers, snowshoers, and walkers. This road gets so much use that it is often packed to the point where snowshoes are not needed. However, exploring north or south from The Elbow on the Long Trail or a traverse of the beaver swamp will require snowshoes. If this hike had a proper trailhead, it would be a near-perfect, easy family snowshoe. As it is, however, the choices are between a road walk, extra mileage or a possible parking ticket.

GETTING THERE: To reach the actual trailhead in Mendon, take U.S. 4 for 6.2 mi. east from U.S. 7 in Rutland or 2.9 mi. west from Sherburne Pass and turn north on the paved Old Turnpike Road. Marble Valley Regional Transit busses from Rutland and Killington serve this junction a dozen times per day in winter. The trailhead is 1.7 mi. up the Old Turnpike Road, after it turns to gravel, at a snowplow turnaround. Unfortunately, there is no legal parking at the turnaround, and the local police are watchful. There are two legal choices. Either walk from U.S. 4 or request permission at the Cortina Inn, 0.8 mi. east of the Old Turnpike Road junction, to park and hike its approximately 0.5 mi. snowmobile trail to a point on the Old Turnpike Rd. about 0.1 mi. west of the Canty Trail's beginning, then hike a mile up the Old Turnpike Road.

DESCRIPTION: From the end of the plowed road (0.0 mi.), the Old Turnpike Road continues straight ahead down a gentle hill. As it climbs up the other side, the remains of a kiln that predates 1869 can be seen about 70 ft. to the right in the hardwoods. The top of the rise is at 2,020 ft. This point, in the gap between Mt. Willard and Blue Ridge Mtn., is the highest elevation on the old road. At the bottom of the hill, a small indentation in the snow on the right indicates the remains of a homestead from the 1800s. By now, the Catamount Trail has joined the road. After passing two large, modern camps on the left, the road narrows and descends somewhat steeply to an area of former beaver ponds. Very soon after crossing a small brook, it passes a mound on the right, site of another old foundation. Soon the road passes through a little cut. To the left, the unplowed Wildcat Road, and Catamount Trail, leads across an old beaver pond toward Chittenden. Straight ahead, the original turnpike continues into an old beaver swamp. To the right, a logging road built in 2002 bypasses the swamp. Taking the drier, less adventurous route, the right fork eventually rejoins the old turnpike for a short climb to The Elbow, where the Long Trail crosses. This is 1.4 mi. from the snowplow turnaround, involving about 100 ft. of climbing and is actually a few feet lower than the start of the trail. The old turnpike now descends steeply to the east and in a half mile, reaches an abandoned four corners. The left (north) turn leads 0.5 mi. to another homestead foundation. Straight ahead, an old Cape Cod-style house is reached in 0.4 mi. The road up from North Sherburne may be plowed that far.

PLEASE REFER TO THE MAP ON PAGE 98

GORHAM LODGE
1950
GREEN MOUNTAIN CLUB

ATTENTION
HIKERS

*A snowshoe doubles as a shovel while removing snow from the door front
at the former Gorham Lodge.*

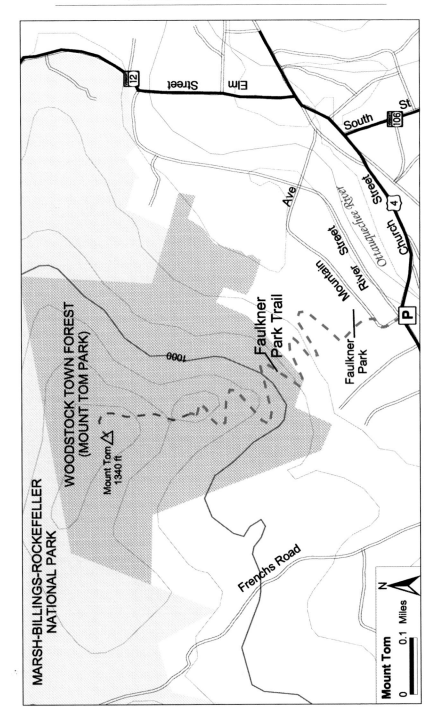

MARSH-BILLINGS-ROCKEFELLER NATIONAL PARK

WOODSTOCK TOWN FOREST (MOUNT TOM PARK)

Mount Tom 1340 ft

1000

Faulkner Park Trail

Faulkner Park

Mountain Street

River Street

Ottauquechee River

Church Street

Ave

South

St

Elm Street

Street

Frenchs Road

P

N

Mount Tom

0   0.1 Miles

12

106

4

㊷ Mount Tom

Location: Woodstock
Distance: 1.0 mi.
Elevation Gain: 600 ft.

Mt. Tom is an easy walk, especially appropriate for beginners and small children, with a rewarding view of Woodstock and east into New Hampshire. The wide trails are part of the Marsh-Billings-Rockefeller National Historic Park. They are free to the public in summer, but are groomed as cross country ski trails in winter and a fee is charged for their use, whether for skiing or snowshoeing. A trail map is available at the park headquarters and the fee may be paid at the Woodstock Inn. There is no fee for the trail described here as it is in a town-owned park.

GETTING THERE: From the Green in Woodstock, travel west on U.S. 4, crossing the river to a three-way intersection with U.S. 4, River Street and Mountain Avenue. On the south side of U.S. 4 is a small parking area at the community center, a two-story building with a slate roof.

DESCRIPTION: From the parking area (0.0 mi.), the route crosses U.S. 4 and follows Mountain Avenue 0.1 mi. to the open area of Faulkner Park on the left. It enters the woods on the back left side of the open area, curving right at a bench and following switchbacks uphill. The trail bears left at two intersections with the Link Trail, which is difficult to follow in winter. At the halfway point, a stone bridge can be seen above. The trail continues its gentle switchback climb, finally ending at a flat area with two benches for admiring the view east into New Hampshire and through the trees down to Woodstock. A sign indicates the summit is 100 yds. further. This last climb to the summit is steep and narrow in places, gaining only a moderate view to the south and west.

Southern Vermont

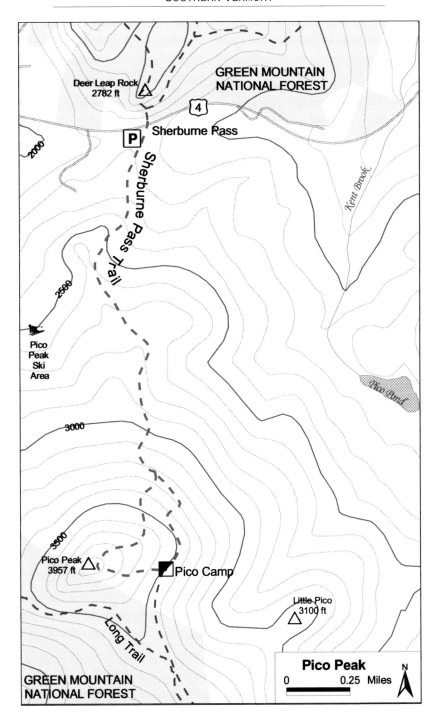

43 Pico Peak

Location: Killington
Distance: 2.5 mi.
Elevation Gain: 1,250 ft.

Conical Pico Peak, the second highest in the Coolidge Range, is most easily reached by the Sherburne Pass Trail. This was the Long Trail until 1999, when it and the Appalachian Trail were moved west of Pico Peak to avoid planned ski area expansion. The round trip to Pico Camp should take about three hours if the trail has been snowshoed recently. The round trip from Pico Camp to Pico Peak, though only 0.8 mi., involves another 600 ft. of climb and probably will take an hour, even if the snow is not so deep as to require crawling under the evergreen branches.

GETTING THERE: The trailhead for this popular hike is on U.S. 4 at the top of Sherburne Pass, east of Rutland. Use the plowed lot on the south side of U.S. 4 opposite the Inn at Long Trail.

DESCRIPTION: From the south end of the parking lot (0.0 mi.), the blue-blazed Sherburne Pass Trail, maintained by the Killington Section of the Green Mountain Club, follows an old road toward Pico Pond then, 0.1 mi. from U.S. 4, turns right to climb to the hardwood ridge. At 0.7 mi., an unmarked but likely tracked trail branches right. It leads about 100 ft. to a Pico Ski Area service road, which reaches the top of a short ski lift, with a good view, in 0.1 mi. The next half-mile of trail can be hard to follow, especially when high wind from west to east has plastered snow over the blazes and masked the trail contours. At first the trail angles along the west side of the ridge, then, at 1.1 mi., it crosses into a nearly flat area on the east side. In the next 0.3 mi., old, weathered insulator posts can be seen on large yellow birches or hemlocks. There are at least four sets, which held the wires for the Pico Peak fire tower telephone. The tower was moved to Killington Peak in the mid 1960s. At 1.3 mi., there are two sinkholes just to the right of the trail. The first opened up only in the late 1990s, while the second, much larger, has been there probably for centuries. A small brook disappears into the larger one. The trail crosses some small brooks and, after three switchbacks, emerges onto Pico's Summit Glades Ski Trail at 2.1 mi., with fine views west to the Adirondacks and north along the Green Mountains. The hiking trail stays to the left (east) edge of the ski trail as it climbs 150 ft. uphill, then turns left into the evergreens. At 2.5 mi., after a fairly level, but steep side hill, the trail passes a spring and reaches the enclosed Pico Camp, with views to the east and southeast. All windows and doors should be latched upon leaving.

From Pico Camp, there are two choices. One possibility is to snow-shoe up the Pico Link hiking trail, which is steep, narrow and overhung with evergreens. At 0.1 mi., it crosses a wide road built to service the Alpine Pipeline. The trail continues uphill into the woods a little to the left of where it entered the road. At 0.3 mi., it emerges onto another ser-vice road, follows it a few feet left, and re-enters the woods. In 100 ft., it enters the 49er Ski Trail, turns left (south), passes left of the top of the ski lift, climbs wooden stairs to the right of a warming hut, and reaches the summit at 0.4 mi. Returning, it is possible to descend the 49er and then the Summit Glades Ski Trail 0.4 mi. back to where the trail first came out onto the Summit Glades Trail below Pico Camp.

Another choice at Pico Camp is to continue south on the nearly level Sherburne Pass Trail 0.2 mi. to the Alpine Pipeline service road already mentioned. It affords wide views from southeast to northeast. The Sher-burne Pass Trail continues another 0.2 mi. south to Jungle Junction, where it ends at the Long Trail/Appalachian Trail, which leads 3.9 mi. north to a point on U.S. 4 one mile west of Sherburne Pass. The Long Trail is unlikely to be well snowshoed as far up as Jungle Junction, which means a long afternoon of route-finding and trail breaking often through deep snow.

Snowshoers at a GMC camp in 1917.

44 Clarendon Loop

Location: Clarendon
Distance: 2.0 mi.
Elevation Gain: 600 ft.

This simple loop hike provides challenging terrain, an expansive vista and a gentle ridge walk for a half day's effort. To visit Clarendon Gorge, follow the Long Trail as it descends from the east end of the parking area. The suspension bridge over the gorge was built by Green Mountain Club volunteers in 1974, after the previous bridge and its northern abutment were swept away by the 1973 floods. The trail and bridge timbers may be icy.

GETTING THERE: The parking lot for the Long Trail/Appalachian Trail is on Vt. 103, 2.4 mi. east of U.S. 7 in Clarendon and 6.0 miles west of Vt. 155 in East Wallingford. The parking area may not be plowed in deep snow.

DESCRIPTION: The loop hike starts by crossing Vt. 103 at the railroad crossing (0.0 mi.). It descends the road embankment and encounters the first of many challenges: a stile. Stiles are intended to let hikers pass without letting farm animals out of their fenced enclosures. Once a staple of the Appalachian Trail in New England, stiles are disappearing as agricultural use of trail lands wanes. The trail crosses a small field to another stile, then climbs through a power line clearing to the base of a slot ravine at the foot of the ledges. The ravine can be a challenge and snowshoes with crampons provide a definite advantage. The climb is direct and can be rewarded with animal tracks in the snow, maybe even a bobcat. At the top of the ravine, the trail bears right and ascends gently to a lookout (0.4 mi.) where there is a view of Clarendon Gorge and Mill River. From this lookout, the trail follows the ridgeline on easy grades before descending to the abandoned Gaynor Road (1.0 mi.), which was once the route of the Long Trail, and the open-faced Clarendon Shelter just beyond. Bearing right from the front of the shelter, the trail rejoins the old road south, following the old Long Trail back to Vt. 103. At about the halfway point, an old woods road enters from the left. This was once part of the Old Crown Point Road, a military route used by the colonists to support Fort Ticonderoga during the French and Indian War. The trail continues downhill, crosses a brook, passes under the power line and returns to Vt. 103 (2.0 mi.).

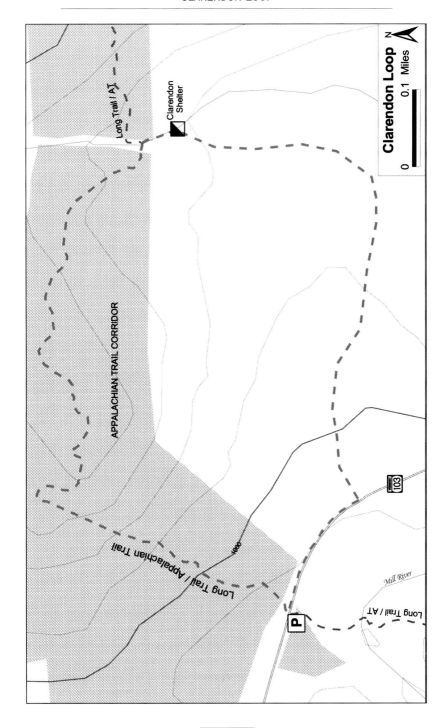

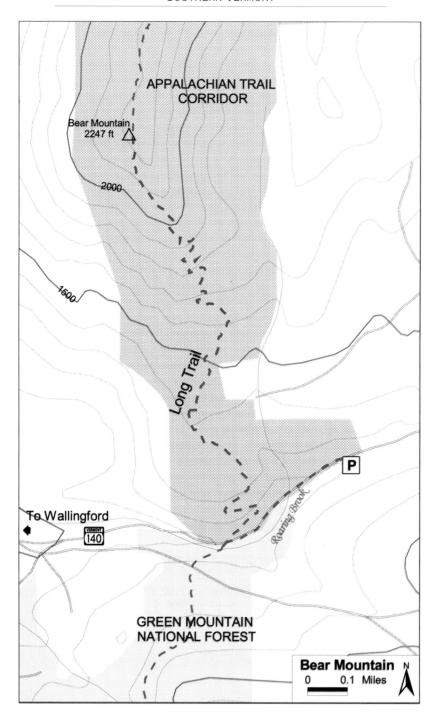

㊺ Bear Mountain

Location: Wallingford
Distance: 4.0 mi.
Elevation Gain: 800 ft.

The Long Trail crosses Bear Mtn. north of Vt. 140, the Wallingford Gulf Road. The mountain's best feature is a domed ledge 1.1 mi. from Vt. 140, from which there are excellent views to the south, including White Rocks. While the ledge makes a good turnaround for a shorter hike, climbing to the summit, though steep and difficult, does offer other good views as well.

GETTING THERE: The Long Trail crosses Vt. 140, 2.7 mi. east of Wallingford and 3.6 mi. west of East Wallingford. There is no winter parking at the Long Trail crossing, nor at the summer trailhead parking lot off Vt. 140. Parking for several cars is usually available at the Sugar Hill Road, which is 2.1 mi. east of the village of Wallingford and 0.5 mi. east of the Long Trail crossing on Vt. 140. Parking for 2-3 cars is usually available at a pull-off 0.4 mi. east of the trail, and parking for 1-2 cars is occasionally available at a pull-off 0.2 mi. east of Wallingford. The road walk is actually interesting because it goes through the narrowest part of rocky Wallingford Gulf.

DESCRIPTION: From Vt. 140 (0.0 mi.), the white-blazed Long Trail heads uphill through evergreens and the summer parking lot, following an old farm road that angles to the west up the hillside. At 0.2 mi., it switchbacks to the east and, in about 50 ft., crosses a stone wall, climbs slightly through an overgrown field, crosses another stone wall and enters a more overgrown area. About 100 ft. to the east is what appears to be the foundation of a barn. The trail crosses another stonewall, follows it to the west, turns north from it, and ascends gradually about 100 ft. east of an open ledge with a view of White Rocks. At 0.6 mi., it crosses another stone wall to enter the Bear Mtn. Road, abandoned at this point. This was the original route from Wallingford to East Wallingford. Although hilly, it probably was an easier road to build than the current one through the gulf on Vt. 140, at least with the equipment of the late 1700s. In 50 ft., the trail turns left (north) from the road (this turn is easy to miss in winter) and enters open hardwood forest where the trail is particularly hard to find when snow is on the ground. The blazes are, however, always within sight of each other. The trail now passes west of a huge boulder and, at 0.9 mi., enters an old road leading from the Bear Mtn. Road north to Patch Hollow. In a few feet, it turns left from the road and passes through an abandoned orchard. The trail climbs over several switchbacks and, at one point where it reverses direction from west to east, a blue-blazed side trail leads about 300 ft. to the domed ledge with excellent views south, including White Rocks. The ledge, with an elevation of about 1,575 ft., is 1.1 mi. from Vt. 140. At 1.5 mi., the trail reaches the ridge of Bear Mtn, then, without a lot more climbing, attains the Long Trail's highest point on Bear Mtn., 2,100 ft. (2.1 mi.). The Long Trail descends north from here into Patch Hollow.

A group of snowshoers enjoying a break at Taft Lodge, 1940.

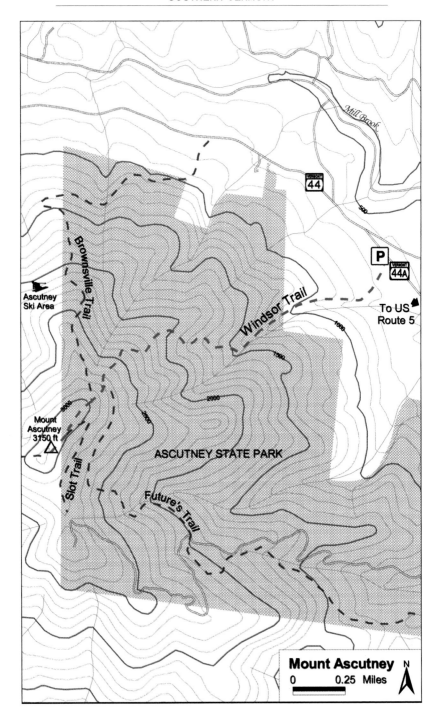

Mount Ascutney
0   0.25 Miles
N

46 Mount Ascutney

Location: Windsor
Distance: 2.8 mi.
Elevation Gain: 2,520 ft.

A monadnock, Mt. Ascutney is a dominant feature of the Connecticut River Valley in southeastern Vermont. It offers 360-degree views from an observation tower, as well as pleasant views from lookouts on the trail. It is climbed by four foot trails and an auto road, which is unplowed and snowmobiled in winter. The Windsor Trail, described here, begins at a plowed parking lot and has a fairly consistent grade, as well as a northeast exposure, which generally holds snow well, though about a half mile near the bottom is exposed to the south and loses snow early. All of the foot trails on Mt. Ascutney have steep pitches and should only be attempted with snowshoes that have creepers or crampons, unless snow conditions are unusually forgiving. There are often ski tracks made by telemarkers meandering around the upper mountain, so it pays to watch carefully for blazes, signs and landmarks. The foot trails are maintained by volunteer members of the Ascutney Trails Association, established in 1967. The group publishes a guidebook, describing the trails in detail and giving both historical and natural history information of the area. It is available from the association at P.O. Box 147, Windsor VT 05089 or from the Green Mountain Club.

GETTING THERE: From Exit 8 on Interstate 91, turn east on Vt. 131 for a short distance to U.S. 5. Turn north on U.S. 5, follow it 1.1 mi. to Vt. 44A and turn left. Follow Vt. 44A past Ascutney State Park (2.3 mi.) to the parking lot on the left side of the road (4.0 mi.), which is marked by an ATA sign on the right side of the road.

DESCRIPTION: Leaving the parking lot (0.0 mi.), the white-blazed Windsor Trail follows the southern boundary of an open field, where it is shaded by conifers on the upper end and soon joins a woods road. It begins an increasingly steep climb in open hardwoods on the north side of the ravine of Mountain Brook. For nearly 0.5 mi., the slope of the ravine, which faces south, receives as much sun as the equator, so snow cover may be thin or absent. The trail crosses the right branch of the brook (0.9 mi.), then follows the left branch upstream a short distance before swinging to the right and slabbing westerly to recross the right branch (1.1 mi.). It continues over and around a low shoulder of the mountain to reach a junction at Halfway Spring (1.6 mi.), the former site of a loggers' cabin, where the trail splits. The left fork, the main trail, follows a route cut in 1903 to replace the original 1857 route, which was ruined by an 1888 forest fire that burned the humus layer. The right fork leads to a spring and log shelter with a stone fireplace, built by the ATA in 1968. The two routes then rejoin to climb steeply to the upper junction with the Blood Rock Trail (2.0 mi.). The trail passes junctions with the Futures Trail on the left (2.2 mi.) and with a short spur trail to Castle Rock (2.4 mi.), where there is a view of the Connecticut River Valley, also on the left. At the next junction, the Brownsville Trail enters from the right and the two coincide for the final ascent to the small open area at the Stone Hut site. To the right, a short spur leads to massive Brownsville Rock, where there are extensive views of much of the Green Mountain Range. As the trail climbs atop the ridge, it passes a junction on the left with the Slot Trail, which descends to the Mountain Road parking lot. The Windsor/ Brownsville Trail continues through the woods, passes the observation tower and soon reaches a junction with the Weathersfield Trail at a short spur trail to the summit (2.8 mi.). Two communications towers fill the mountain's highest point, making the views from the summit mediocre. The views are better from the observation tower. A cabin and tower were originally constructed on the summit in 1920 for forest fire surveillance. The Civilian Conservation Corps built a new steel tower from 1938 to 1940 and the site remained operational until 1952 when airplane fire patrols were established. The CCC tower was dismantled in 1988 and today's 24.5-ft. observation tower was constructed with an open deck by the State of Vermont in 1989, using steel elements from the old tower. It affords panoramic views from treetop level of New Hampshire's White Mountains, Vermont's Green Mountains, Massachusetts's Berkshires and Vermont's Taconics.

Snowshoeing is a wonderful way for the whole family to enjoy winter.

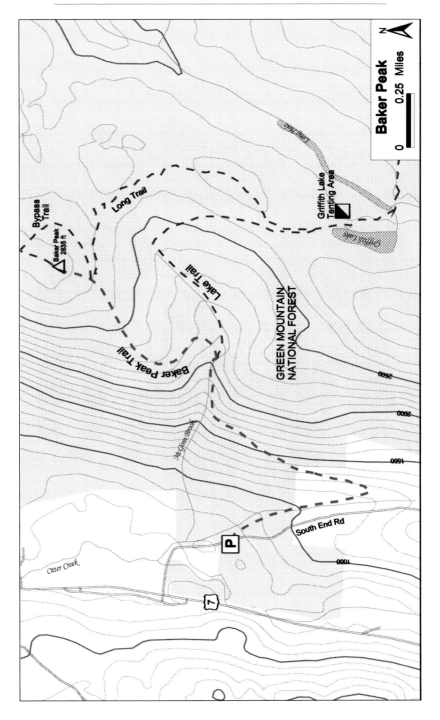

⓸⓻ Baker Peak

Location: Mount Tabor
Distance: 2.9 mi.
Elevation Gain: 2,200 ft.

At 2,850 ft., Baker Peak is far from the highest of the Green Mountains, but it offers near-panoramic views. The lower two thirds of the climb follow the blue-blazed Lake Trail, an old road cut in the late 19th century to reach a lodge on Griffith Lake built by lumber baron Silas Griffith, who owned vast tracts in the area. A number of Griffiths lie in the cemetery at the turn off U.S. 7 onto South End Road. Silas Griffith's Lake House is long since gone, but the old road survives surprisingly intact and makes for good snowshoeing except when there is a crust on the steeper sidehill stretches where the road has eroded into a two-foot wide path. To play it safe, use snowshoes with crampons.

GETTING THERE: To reach the trailhead, turn off U.S. 7 east onto South End Road in the Town of Mt. Tabor. This intersection is 2.0 mi. south of the crossroad from Danby Village to Mt. Tabor Village and is 2.5 mi. north of North Dorset. Follow the paved South End Road 0.5 mi. to a U.S. Forest Service trailhead parking lot on the left, usually plowed in winter.

DESCRIPTION: From the parking area (0.0 mi.), the Lake Trail follows an old road as it climbs south through beautiful, tall white pines. Occasional barbed wire along the left side shows this was once pasture. The road briefly descends to cross a brook, which while normally small, can be hard to cross if the water is high. The road then parallels the brook and soon crosses a short wet stretch. At 0.7 mi., the road forks and the route follows the left fork, which now climbs gradually to the north. The right fork passes a small pond on the right, an indication that the left-fork turn has been missed. At 0.9 mi., the Lake Trail enters the Big Branch Wilderness and the blazes become infrequent. The Danby marble quarries can soon be seen on the opposite side of the valley as well as the meanders of Otter Creek some 700 ft. below. The trail crosses a nicely built footbridge (1.5 mi.) anchored onto a rock face. Pieces of solid barstock cemented into the rock, which apparently once supported a much larger bridge, can still be seen. Once the road begins to turn east into the ravine of McGinn Brook, there is a very obscure junction (1.6 mi.) where an unmarked spur trail climbs about 175 ft. right to a fine view up and down the Great Valley of Vermont and across it to the marble quarries and Dorset Peak. The spur traverses a steep slope, which may be difficult even on snowshoes with crampons. The first major view from the old road itself occurs at a sharp bend around a second rock face, which is visible from U.S. 7, especially in the winter. To this point, fox, coyote and other tracks may be seen in the snow. At the head of the ravine, the trail crosses the brook and immediately turns left (north) away from the Lake Trail, which continues up the old Griffith road to the Long Trail north of Griffith Lake. Depending on ice accumulation and flow, this brook crossing may be difficult for people and dogs. The ascent to this point is about 1,300 ft. From the brook crossing (1.9 mi.), the route follows the Baker Peak Trail northeasterly, with a moderate grade, mostly on old logging roads. There is one sharp, poorly marked right turn at a big yellow birch, from which the trail then goes straight up the hill 500 ft. to another old woods road where it continues back to the left. The Baker Peak Trail ends at the Long Trail (2.8 mi.). From here, the route to the summit turns left (north) to follow the white-blazed Long Trail. A sign marks the blue blazed bad-weather by-pass to the right, which swings to the east of and eventually around to the north side of the summit. While part of this trail passes through evergreens that may not give much clearance if the snow is deep, it may still be easier than clambering over alternating snow and rock on the Long Trail itself. To the west are views of the Great Valley of Vermont, Danby and the Adirondacks; to the north are Pico and Killington Peaks. To the southeast is the ridge of Peru Peak, with the Stratton Mtn. fire tower just behind it. To the south and west are the two highest peaks in the Taconics, Equinox and Dorset, and in the valley in front of them is Emerald Lake, just north of the source of Otter Creek, which meanders its way north to Lake Champlain.

Snowshoeing made easy on a well packed trail.

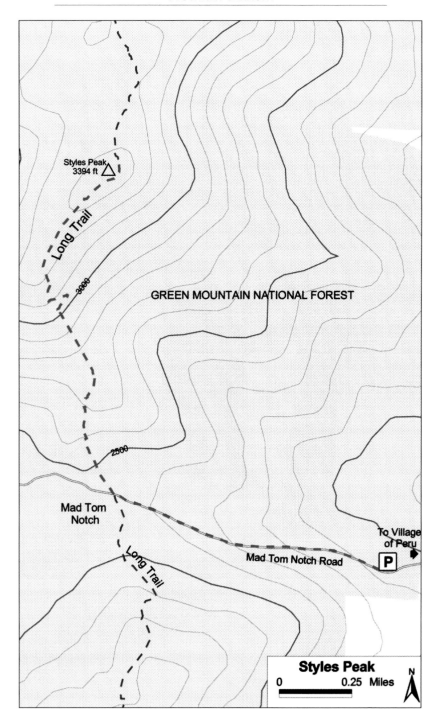

Styles Peak
3394 ft

Long Trail

GREEN MOUNTAIN NATIONAL FOREST

3000

2500

Mad Tom
Notch

Long Trail

To Village
of Peru

Mad Tom Notch Road

P

Styles Peak

0   0.25   Miles

N

48 Styles Peak

Location: Peru
Distance: 5.2 mi.
Elevation gain: 1,100 ft.

Everyone wonders for whom Mad Tom Notch was named. The most plausible explanation is that the term "Mad Tom" did not refer to a person, but was 19th century slang for a type of fish found in mountain brooks. The Long Trail/Appalachian Trail crosses the Notch between North Bromley Mtn. and the Styles Peak/Peru Peak ridge in the Peru Peak Wilderness. On most days in winter, the last part of the climb to Styles Peak is windy and much colder than in Mad Tom Notch.

GETTING THERE: From Vt. 11, turn into the village of Peru (3.5 mi. east of the junction of Vt. 11 and Vt. 30 and 4.4 mi. west of the junction of Vt. 11 and Vt. 100). From the J.J. Hapgood Store in the center of the village follow the Hapgood Pond Road 1.0 mi., turn left onto North Road. From North Road take the second left onto Mad Tom Notch Road, which is also U.S. Forest Service Road 21. Follow this 1.1 mi. to a large parking lot on the right. This is the winter use lot, which is used primarily by snowmobilers. Park appropriately so that those with trailers can share the lot.

DESCRIPTION: From the winter parking lot (0.0 mi.), the hike begins with a 1.0 mi. trek up the snowmobile trail following U.S Forest Service Road 21 to the height of land. This is a side trail in the VAST system and usually not busy. At the height of land, the route turns right to follow the white-blazed Long Trail north to the summit of Styles Peak. This trail is in wilderness so the blazes are spaced far apart and are easily obscured by both blown snow packed on the sides of trees and deep snow near the summit. The Long Trail begins fairly level, passing the Wilderness boundary in 0.1 mi., then gently rising through hardwood forest. It climbs several short, steep pitches alternating with level stretches. These can be challenging when conditions are either icy or the snow deep. At 1.8 mi., the trail climbs the steepest part of Styles Peak in long switch-backs. This is a pleasant section, winding through open hardwoods, with excellent views to the south and southeast. The tower on Bromley Mtn. is visible, with the top of Stratton Mtn. just behind it. After the last switchback, the trail levels, then begins the final climb to the top through first a mix of spruce and yellow birch, then spruce forest. The trail is mostly level with some short moderate climbs and one short downhill. It passes between narrow rocks and trends uphill for another 0.1 mi. to the rocky summit of Styles Peak, where there is a view east over the Landgrove Valley to Glebe Mtn., Okemo Mtn., Mt. Ascutney and, on a clear day, to New Hampshire. The Long Trail continues north to Peru Peak and Griffith Lake.

Snowshoeing in 1993 at the GMC Snowshoe Festival.

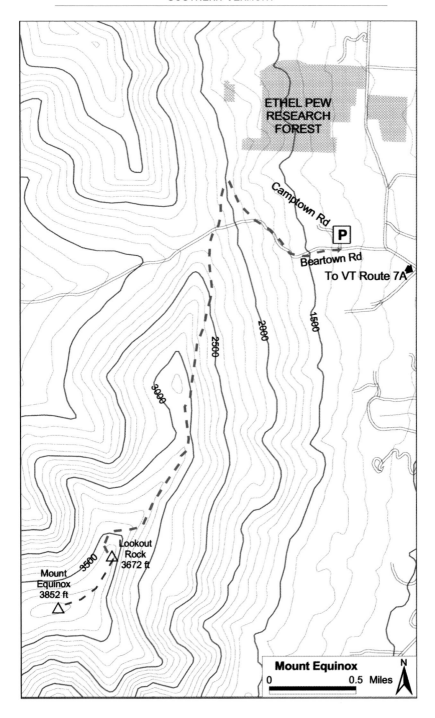

49 Mount Equinox

Location: Manchester Center
Distance: 3.5 mi.
Elevation Gain: 2,300 ft.

The views from the trail are good for most of this hike and especially from Lookout Rock. Despite that, the trail is rarely crowded.

GETTING THERE: From Manchester Center, take Vt. 7A south to Manchester Village. At the Mark Skinner Library, make a 45-degree right turn on West Road. Follow West Road 2.0 miles to a left turn on Three Maple Drive. Take the second left on Beartown Road, then turn right just before the end of the plowing, on Camptown Road, which is a private road/driveway. The owner allows hikers to park here as long as they do not block the driveway.

DESCRIPTION: The hike begins on the unplowed Beartown Road (0.0 mi.) and follows it 0.5 mi. to a fork. It takes the left fork, which climbs steeply at first, then more gently to a T-junction (0.7 mi.) with a heavily used snowmobile trail. The trail turns left and trends generally uphill at easy to moderate grades. At the crest of the hill, a sign reminds people not to vandalize the privately owned land. Here, the trail turns left and after 0.2 mi. swings onto a narrow track, which sidehills up the east side of the ridge for 0.8 mi. The forest remains open, mature hardwoods with excellent views down the Great Valley of Vermont and over to Stratton, Bromley and Magic Mtns. At the top of the ridge, the trail turns left (south) to follow the ridgeline, first briefly downhill, then gently uphill for 1.2 mi. Along this ridge, the forest transitions from hardwoods to spruce. The trail leaves the top of the ridge to continue climbing just below on the west side. As the trail again nears the top of the ridge, a faint trail on the left leads to Lookout Rock. Fifty feet further, another faint trail, marked by a small sign facing the other direction, also leads to Lookout Rock (3.5 mi.). From Lookout Rock, on a clear day, it is possible to see Magic, Bromley, Okemo, and Ascutney Mtns. in the east, as well as New Hampshire's Monadnock, Cardigan and Sunapee Mtns. To the south are Mt. Snow, Haystack, Stratton and Glastenbury Mtns. and Massachusetts's Mt. Greylock. To the north are Styles, Peru and Shrewsbury Peaks. The trail continues 0.3 mi. to the summit of Mt. Equinox.

㊿ Lye Brook Falls

Location: Manchester
Distance: 2.2 mi.
Elevation Gain: 900 ft.

Lye Brook Falls are beautiful, whether running or frozen, but they are especially spectacular at the beginning of the spring snowmelt. The series of cascades is one of the highest in Vermont.

GETTING THERE: From U.S. 7, take exit 4 and turn east on Vt. 11/30 for 0.3 mi. Turn sharply right on East Manchester Road and follow it 1.2 mi. to a left on Glen Road. From here, Glen Road is sometimes passable with a four-wheel drive vehicle. If not, it is possible to park here, being careful not to block either Bensen Road or Glen Road.

DESCRIPTION: The trailhead is 0.4 mi. straight ahead on Glen Road. At the summer parking lot, a small sign in the back of the lot reads 'Trail' (0.0 mi.). The blue-blazed trail passes the U.S. Forest Service sign for the Lye Brook Trail 100 ft. from the parking lot. The trail bears right, then left, reaching a view of the river just before the trail register. From the sign for the Lye Brook Wilderness, the trail mostly follows the raised embankment of a logging railroad built in 1914 to reach the timber in what is now wilderness. While the trail crosses the wilderness area, it is narrower and there are fewer blazes. The trail now trends gently up-hill and Mt. Equinox can be seen on the right. As the trail reaches the first softwoods, it begins a long, steady climb. Hardwoods alternate with hemlock stands, and wherever the high forest canopy is open, young hemlock trees encroach on the trail. At 1.8 mi., the trail levels for 100 yds., coming to a fork, both tines of which are blue-blazed. About 10 ft. up in a tree, a sign marked 'Falls' includes an arrow pointing to the right. The trail to the falls bears right, following the arrow, descending gently across the hillside on the bed of the old railroad. It is narrow with a steep drop-off on the right, and ends at the falls (2.2 mi.). Until 1920, a high trestle carried logging trains across the ravine below the falls. On the return, about 100 yds. downhill from the fork in the trail, the stone retaining wall supporting the rail bed will be visible above.

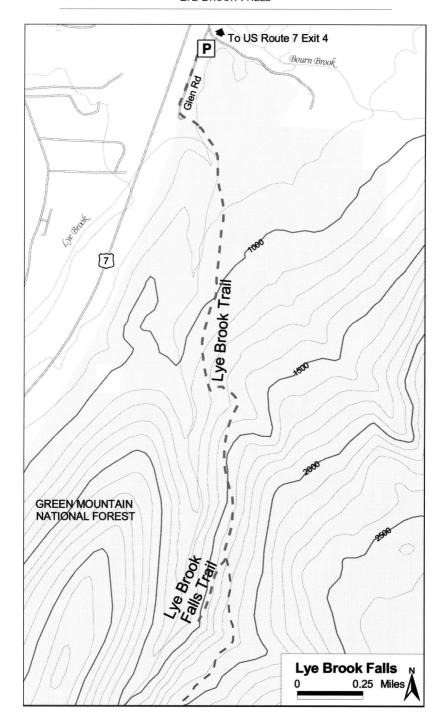

To US Route 7 Exit 4

P

Glen Rd

Bourn Brook

Lye Brook

7

1000

Lye Brook Trail

1500

2000

GREEN MOUNTAIN
NATIONAL FOREST

2500

Lye Brook
Falls Trail

Lye Brook Falls N

0   0.25 Miles

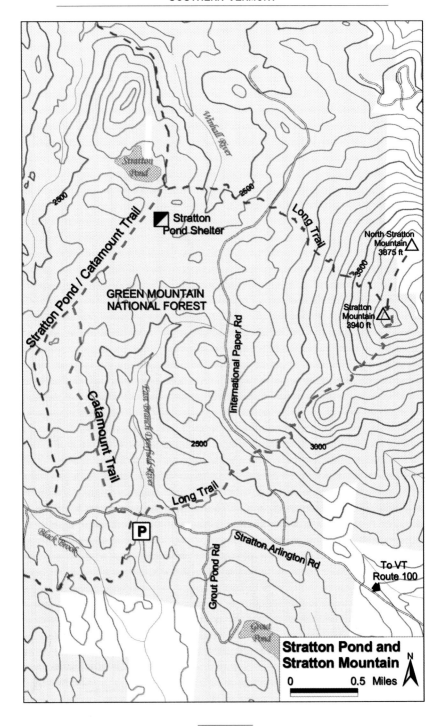

Stratton Pond
Stratton
Pond Shelter
Stratton Pond / Catamount Trail
Catamount Trail
Long Trail
North Stratton
Mountain
3875 ft
Stratton
Mountain
3940 ft
GREEN MOUNTAIN
NATIONAL FOREST
International Paper Rd
East Branch Deerfield River
2500
3000
Long Trail
P
Black Brook
Grout Pond Rd
Stratton Arlington Rd
To VT
Route 100
Grout
Pond

Stratton Pond and Stratton Mountain

0   0.5 Miles

N

🗐 Stratton Pond

Location: Stratton
Distance: 3.7 mi.
Elevation Gain: 400 ft.

From Stratton Pond, which is often solid enough to walk across in winter, the views of Stratton Mountain are unsurpassed. The three-sided shelter near the pond offers both a place for lunch and overnight camping, although no open fires are allowed. Since this is a shared trail, it is important to wear either skis or snowshoes to avoid postholing (wearing only boots and sinking into the snow leaving deep holes), which makes the trail difficult if not dangerous for skiers.

GETTING THERE: From Vt. 100 in West Wardsboro, 8.5 mi. south of the junction of Vt. 100 and Vt. 30 or 13.6 mi. north of the junction of Vt. 100 and Vt. 9, travel west on the Stratton-Arlington Road 6.8 mi. to the Long Trail parking lot on the right (north) side at the end of the plowed road. This lot is shared by snowmobilers, skiers and hikers. On weekends, a "chuck wagon" may be parked in the lot selling hot chocolate, hot dogs and chili.

DESCRIPTION: From the parking lot (0.0 mi.), the route, which is marked with the Catamount Trail's blue diamonds, follows the snowmobile trail west uphill for 0.25 mi. As the hill levels, the trail leaves the snowmobile route and turns right (north) on an old logging road where it climbs briefly to a Catamount Trail sign-in register. From here, it continues to climb gently to a fork about 1.0 mi. from the parking area. The trail bears left and trends downhill for 1.1 mi. to a junction where it turns right to follow the blue-blazed Stratton Pond Trail. The shared Stratton Pond/Catamount Trail now meanders northeast through mixed hardwoods with little change in elevation. At 3.6 mi., it reaches a signed junction with the trail leading 200 yds. east to Stratton Pond Shelter and in another 500 ft., the signed junction with the Long Trail/Appalachian Trail. The trail to the pond turns left to follow Catamount Trail blazes and white Long Trail blazes 0.1 mi. to the pond (3.7 mi.).

52 Stratton Mountain

Location: Stratton
Distance: 3.8 mi.
Elevation Gain: 1,706 ft.

It was in 1909 on Stratton Mountain, at 3,936 ft. one of the hundred highest peaks in New England and the highest in southern Vermont, that James P. Taylor first had the idea of a hiking trail extending the length of Vermont. In 1921, after construction of the Long Trail had already begun, Benton MacKaye conceived the idea of the Appalachian Trail on Stratton Mtn. Although the summit is wooded, a historic fire tower built by the Civilian Conservation Corps in 1934 provides both views and shelter from the wind. The tower and 1928-vintage fire observer's cabin are listed on the National Register of Historic Places. Because the Long Trail blazes are white, few and far between and anywhere from ankle height to chest height depending on snow depth, the trail to the summit of Stratton can be difficult to follow if untracked.

GETTING THERE: See driving directions for Stratton Pond on page 135.

DESCRIPTION: From the parking lot (0.0 mi.), the Long Trail leaves north on a gentle grade and passes a beaver pond complex on the left at 0.8 mi. At 1.4 mi., it crosses the International Paper Road (unplowed and snow-mobiled). From here, it climbs steadily, then the grade eases as it follows the nearly straight-line course of the long-vanished telephone line that once connected to the fire tower. The trail passes Little Stratton on the right and leads into the col between Little Stratton and Stratton (2.7 mi.). A series of switchbacks climbs to the south peak and fire tower (3.8 mi.). From the tower, there are views in all directions. Directly north is the north peak of Stratton Mtn. and the ski area gondola station; Killington Peak is in the distance. Somerset Reservoir and Mt. Snow are to the south; the Taconics and Mt. Equinox are to the west; Glastenbury Mtn. is southwest; Mt. Ascutney is northeast and New Hampshire's Grand Monadnock is southeast.

PLEASE REFER TO THE MAP ON PAGE 134

Snowshoers negotiate a tricky stream crossing.

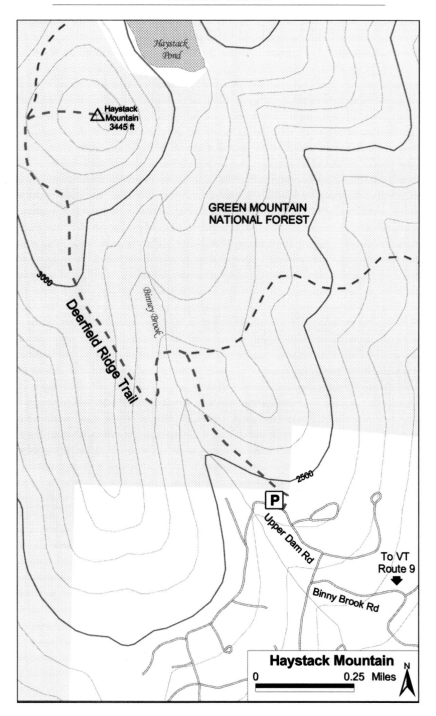

Haystack Mountain

0   0.25 Miles

N

53 Haystack Mountain

Location: Wilmington
Distance: 1.8 mi.
Elevation Gain: 1,025 ft.

This snowshoe trek provides a big mountain feeling for only a moderate amount of effort. While the summit is nearly 3,500 ft. in elevation and cloaked in a high-elevation conifer forest, the amount of climbing is moderate because the trailhead is nearly halfway up the mountain. More than two-thirds of the route is easy winter walking because it's often packed out by snowmobilers, skiers and other snowshoers. However, after a recent snowfall, the occasional blowdowns, infrequent trail markers and absence of previous tracks may make route finding a bit challenging. Winter may be the perfect season to climb Haystack. The water and mud that plague the trail during the warmer months are covered with snow and the groups of visitors that usually crowd the tiny summit are gone.

GETTING THERE: Reaching the trailhead, located in the Chimney Hill development in Wilmington, may be the most difficult route finding of the trip. From the traffic light in Wilmington, travel 1.0 mi. west on Vt. 9 to a right (north) turn on Haystack Road. In 1.25 mi. from Vt. 9, turn left at a large Chimney Hill sign pointing the way to the Clubhouse and Chimney Hill Roads. In 0.15 mi., turn right on the unpaved Binney Brook Road and follow it steeply uphill for 1.0 mi., bearing left at all three forks. At the end of Binney Brook Road, turn right on Upper Dam Road, continue a short distance to a T-intersection and turn left. The trailhead is 0.2 mi. further and is marked by a U.S. Forest Service sign. Parking is on the wide, plowed shoulder of the road, just beyond the trailhead.

DESCRIPTION: From the trailhead (0.0 mi.), the route begins on a wide woods road, ascending gently past a yellow gate to an intersection (0.5 mi.), where numerous signs announce that the lands beyond, which extend to Haystack Pond and the Wilmington water supply, are closed to snowmobiles. The trail turns left, where as of 2005, a small sign with an arrow and the word "top" pointed the way. The now narrower trail, labeled on some maps as the Deerfield Ridge Trail, descends slightly before leveling out. The route is marked sporadically with blue or red diamond-shaped markers and may be shared with snowmobilers for the next mile, although snowmobile traffic is generally light. A blue marker signals a sharp right turn, where the trail climbs steadily for 0.25 mi. to the top of the ridge. The ridge is populated by a forest of interesting-shaped trees. The absence of leaves gives a clear view of contorted beech trees, short, stout yellow birch and ragged-looking red spruce, all indicative of the harsh, windy, icy environment in which these trees survive. The summit of Haystack is visible from one particularly open area. The trail climbs as it passes some steep ledges and comes to a junction (1.5 mi.) where it turns right, off the Deerfield Ridge Trail, at another small sign pointing to the "top." From here, the trail climbs another 300 ft. on a narrow, twisting footpath to the summit clearing, which overlooks much of Windham County. Directly below is Haystack Pond and several towers of the Haystack Mtn. Ski Area can be seen poking through the trees on the hill beyond. Straight ahead is the snow-capped peak of New Hampshire's Mt. Monadnock. To the left, on the far end of the Deerfield Ridge, is Mt. Snow. To the right are several outlooks providing views southeast over Harriman Reservoir and south to Mt. Greylock.

A view of Haystack Mountain from Wantastiquet Mountain.

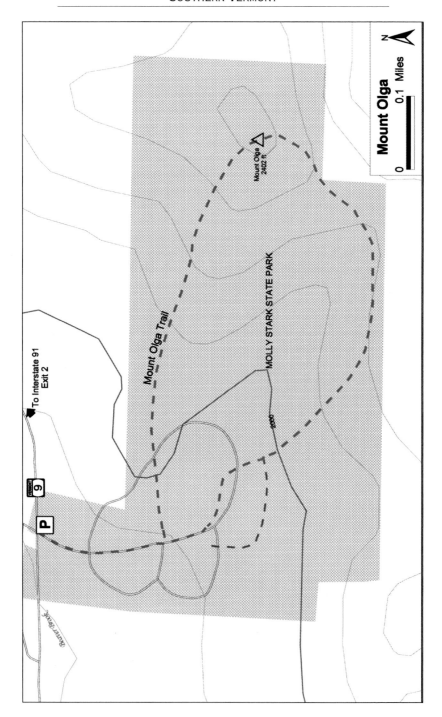

N

Mount Olga

0.1 Miles

0

Mount Olga
2402 ft

MOLLY STARK STATE PARK

2000

Mount Olga Trail

To Interstate 91
Exit 2

VERMONT 9

P

Beaver Brook

54 Mount Olga

Location: Wilmington
Distance: 1.9 mi. loop
Elevation Gain: 514 ft.

Although a hike to the summit of Mt. Olga hardly qualifies as a wilderness experience, it does offer a pleasant 1.9-mi. loop through varied woodlands with far-reaching views from the fire tower. Unlike longer treks, there will be plenty of time to look around and appreciate the attractive woodlands. This is also a great first mountain to climb on snowshoes as the trail is rarely steep and is usually packed out by other snowshoers. In addition, the windows of the fire tower cabin are glazed, so visitors can enjoy the unusual luxury of taking in the views while shielded from the wind. The trail lies within the Molly Stark State Park in Wilmington.

GETTING THERE: The entrance to the park is on the south side of Vt. 9, 15 mi. west of Exit 2 on Interstate 91 in Brattleboro or 3.3 mi. east of the traffic light in the center of Wilmington. The park's entrance road is gated and unplowed and parking along busy Vt. 9 can be difficult, dangerous and possibly illegal. Parking is available at the end of Sparrow Lane. This side road is a right turn just past the park entrance if coming from Brattleboro and a left turn just before the park entrance if coming from Wilmington. Sparrow Lane immediately curves right and ends in a wide cul-de-sac directly across from the park entrance.

DESCRIPTION: From the cul-de-sac on Sparrow Lane (0.0 mi.), the route follows the park road just past the caretaker's house (0.15 mi.), then turns left at a sign for the Mt. Olga Trail. The blue-blazed trail immediately descends to cross a bridge, then climbs moderately through a spruce and balsam fir forest. It levels and passes through refreshingly open woods where flocks of chickadees serenade (0.3 mi.). The trail climbs again to a junction at 0.75 mi., where a sign provides information about the park. The route turns left onto the 0.1-mi. summit spur trail. After a short, steep pitch, this trail moderates and arrives at the summit. The summit is cluttered with several small buildings and a communications tower. It is also a popular snowmobile destination. However, the 360-degree view from the fire tower is inspiring. Close in to the northwest, the obvious pointed peak is Haystack Mtn. with its ski area just to the right of the summit. Farther down the ridge are Mt. Snow's ski trails. The large mass to the right is Stratton Mtn., whose ski trails are hidden from this vantage point, and the south face of Bromley Mtn. is just beyond. The landslide-scarred face of Mt. Greylock is visible to the southwest in Massachusetts. New Hampshire's Mt. Monadnock is the large, isolated peak to the east. The return route begins back at the spur trail junction and leads straight ahead, instead of turning right onto the ascent trail. The trail descends through birch, beech, maple, cherry and ash hardwood forest. It passes through an area of large boulders, swings right, then follows a fairly direct downhill path toward the park campground, crossing a few tiny streams and paralleling a stonewall, most likely buried in snow. At a junction 0.2 mi. from the campground, a side trail signposted to the nature center leaves right. Although an alternate route to the campground, it is less direct and more difficult to follow in winter. The trail turns sharply right into the campground, then right again onto the campground road, which curves left past a picnic pavilion and the caretaker's house.

The sign reads:

MT. OLGA TRAIL
SUMMIT
FIRETOWER   0.8 MI. △

MT OLGA TRAIL
.8 MI ELEVATION 2415'

The trail head at Mt. Olga.

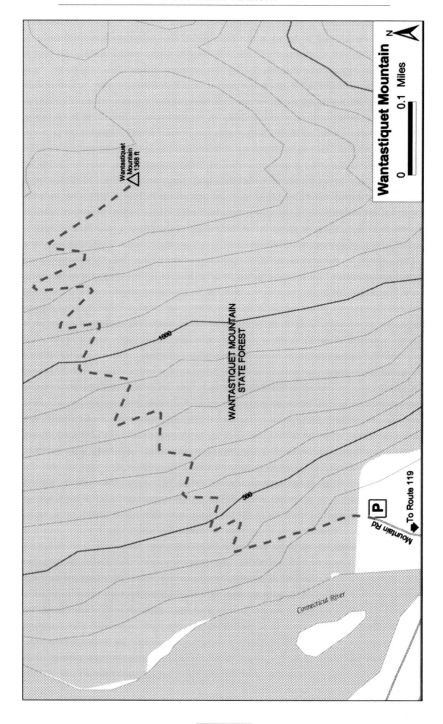

55 Wantastiquet Mountain

Location: New Hampshire
Distance: 1.5 mi.
Elevation Gain: 1018 ft.

Wantastiquet Mtn. may be in New Hampshire, but residents of Brattleboro consider it their own. It rises steeply, more than 1,000 ft. above the Connecticut River and dominates the eastern skyline of the town. Located directly across the river from downtown Brattleboro, the trails are a frequent destination for local residents. Despite its relatively low elevation of 1,350 ft., the rocky summit affords views of many of southern Vermont's major mountains. The 1.5-mi. route follows an old carriage road, eroded in places and with short stretches of bare ground and running water throughout much of the winter. Therefore, any snowshoe trek is more enjoyable after a good snowfall. The short distance makes it possible to hike in the morning and enjoy Brattleboro's vibrant downtown in the afternoon.

GETTING THERE: From the center of Brattleboro, at the corner of Main and High Streets (Vt. 5 and Vt. 9), travel three blocks south and turn left on N.H. 119. Cross the Connecticut River into New Hampshire on a pair of bridges. Just past the second bridge, turn left on Mountain Road and continue to the end, where a parking lot, possibly unplowed, is on the right. Alternatively, it is possible to park in the Wal-Mart parking lot, which is on N.H. 119 just past the turn onto Mountain Road.

DESCRIPTION: From the parking lot (0.0 mi.), the route follows an old road leaving the left side of the lot (not the road that continues straight from the end of Mountain Road). It passes a gate and enters the first two of nine switchbacks that wind up the mountain. Beyond the second switchback is a second gate and a short side trail to the left, leading to a view of downtown Brattleboro. Continuing on the old carriage road, the way is framed by large white pine and hemlock as it climbs gradually to the third switchback, a broad curve to the right, after which the trail steepens. There is likely to be running water and exposed rocks between the fourth and fifth switchbacks. After the fifth, the trail becomes almost flat, climbing again after the sixth. It steepens beyond the seventh as the terrain becomes more rocky and rugged. At the ninth, and final switchback, the north end of Brattleboro is visible over the trees as the trail curves right for the final stretch to the summit. Boulders and rock outcrops line the trail, as does vegetation not commonly found in Vermont, such as pitch pine, red pine and mountain laurel. After the last switchback, a side trail on the right leads a few yards to the summit where there is a large granite marker with a monument to Brattleboro resident Walter Childs who was instrumental in the construction of the carriage road up the mountain in 1890. The view from the summit is special due to its variety. Nearly all of Brattleboro is visible, from its compact downtown with its brick buildings and church steeples to its residential neighborhoods, shopping plazas, rail yards and industrial areas. To the right or northwest, are the Retreat Meadows, which are no longer meadows but a flooded area that, between skating, hockey and ice fishing, is the town's informal winter meeting place. The West River, graced by the arched bridge of Interstate 91, leads the eye off toward Stratton Mtn. The rolling hills, woods and fields give way to mountains such as Haystack and Snow farther on the horizon.